Carrying
Coca

COREGIDOR DE PROVINCIAS
TOCRICOCVESMICHOC

tanbo ynga

corregidor

tocricoc

Carrying Coca

1,500 Years of Andean *Chuspas*

Nicola Sharratt

Published by
Bard Graduate Center: Decorative Arts,
Design History, Material Culture, New York

Distributed by
Yale University Press, New Haven and London

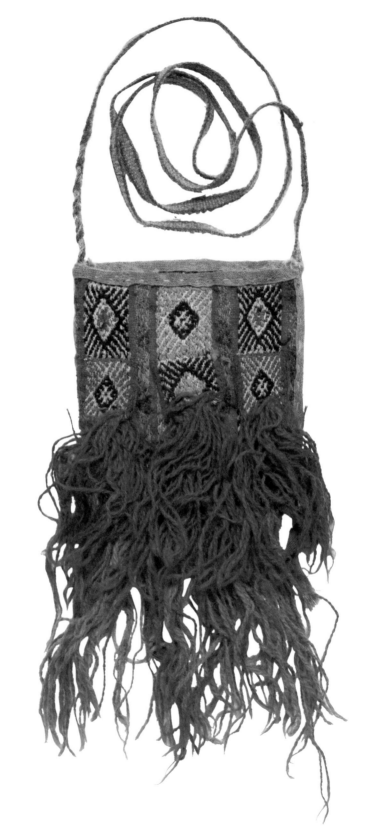

Contents

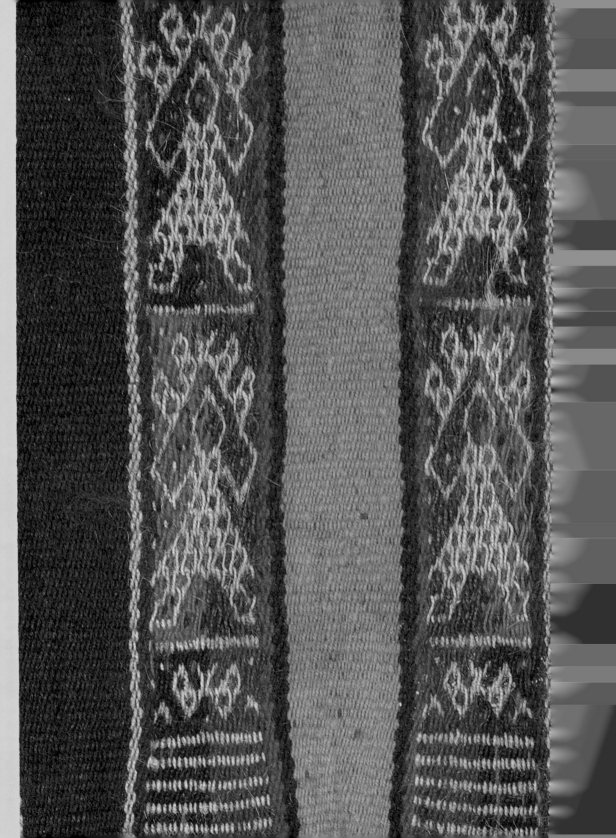

Director's Foreword

The Bard Graduate Center (BGC) and the American Museum of Natural History (AMNH) continue to develop a dynamic and close working relationship. This project, *Carrying Coca*, is the latest in a series of collaborations centered on our joint postdoctoral fellowship program, founded in 2009. Its curator, Nicola Sharratt, is the third scholar to occupy this two-year position and to conceive and complete a Focus Gallery project drawing on the extensive and varied collections of the AMNH's Division of Anthropology.

In *Carrying Coca*, Dr. Sharratt presents a compelling story of Andean inventiveness in a textile form that has persisted for at least 1,500 years: small woven bags for carrying personal supplies of coca leaves. These bags have long played and continue to play complex, practical, and symbolic roles in Andean and neighboring societies. Starting with examples of these bags themselves, Dr. Sharratt shows how they are not merely intricately woven items of personal adornment but are themselves woven into the fabric of social practice and belief, which, while persistent, is not without variety both regionally and over time. She demonstrates that large-scale social changes, such as the growth of the Inca Empire from the fourteenth century on, the arrival of Spanish colonists in the sixteenth century, and the impact of international trade networks and tourism in the twentieth century, have all had discernible effects on bags for carrying coca and on the communities and individuals who use them. She shows that this seemingly modest form, well represented in the collections of the AMNH, has a huge and persistent cultural and social presence.

For her selection of coca bags, Dr. Sharratt has drawn almost exclusively on the AMNH Division of Anthropology collections and, for ancillary material, on the AMNH Research Library Special Collections (Institutional Archives, Manuscripts, and Personal Papers and the Photograph Collection). I wish to acknowledge our debt to Ellen V. Futter, president of the AMNH, for the loans from the museum's collections that have made the exhibition possible. John J. Flynn, dean of the Richard Gilder Graduate School of the AMNH, and Laurel Kendall, chair of the AMNH Division of Anthropology, once again lent invaluable support. Charles Spencer, curator of Mexican and Central American archaeology, took Dr. Sharratt under his wing at the AMNH. Sumru Aricanli, senior scientific assistant for South American archaeology, and Mary Lou Murillo, scientific assistant, kindly facilitated access to the collections for Dr. Sharratt and her students. Kristen Mable, Division of Anthropology registrar for archives and loans, and Barbara Mathé, AMNH archivist and head of Library Special Collections, generously facilitated access to archival materials and the unparalleled collection of museum negatives and films.

As an integral part of this Focus Gallery project, Dr. Sharratt taught the course "Weaving through the Past and into the Present: 10,000 Years of Andean Textiles" (spring 2013) and a workshop (fall 2013). These gave our graduate students outstanding opportunities to familiarize themselves with rich South American cultures and to contribute substantially to the exhibition. The students who participated in the classes or served as assistants and who contributed to the projects are Corinne Brandt, Kelsey Brow, Liz Donato (CUNY), Maeve Hogan, Sophia Lufkin, Sarah Pickman, and Antonio Sánchez Gómez.

The dean of the Bard Graduate Center, Peter Miller, makes the Focus Gallery Project possible through his invaluable support of this collaboration between the Gallery and Academic Programs of the BGC. His attentions are complemented by those of Elena Pinto Simon, dean of Academic Administration and Student Affairs; Nina Stritzler-Levine, director of the Gallery and executive editor of BGC Gallery Publications; and Ivan Gaskell, professor and head of the Focus Gallery Project, who oversaw the endeavor.

Staff members of Academic Programs and the Gallery collaborated to realize Dr. Sharratt's concept: Rebecca Allan, head of Education; Kate DeWitt, art director; Eric Edler, Gallery registrar; Kimon Keramidas, assistant professor and director of the Digital Media Lab; Marianne Lamonaca, associate Gallery director and chief curator; Alexis Mucha, coordinator of catalogue photography; Stephen Nguyen, exhibition preparator; Ian Sullivan, exhibition designer; Ann Marguerite Tartsinis, associate curator and Focus Gallery Project coordinator; and Han Vu, media producer. MediaCombo, led by Robin White Owen, developed the digital interactive that explores the historical and cultural networks of coca and *chuspas* from the pre-Hispanic period to the present. The production of this catalogue was aided by the meticulous work of our copy editor, Barbara Burn, and proofreader, Roberta Fineman. I should like to thank them all, as well as all other members of the faculty and staff of the Bard Graduate Center whose diligent work has made *Carrying Coca* possible.

——Susan Weber
 Director and Founder
 Iris Horowitz Professor in the History of the Decorative Arts
 Bard Graduate Center

Foreword

Nicola Sharratt, Bard Graduate Center and American Museum of Natural History postdoctoral research fellow, 2012–14, brings to the Focus Gallery a discipline hitherto unrepresented: archaeology. As well as being well versed in the theoretical interpretation of excavations, Dr. Sharratt, who completed her doctorate at the University of Illinois at Chicago, came to the BGC from the Field Museum, Chicago, as an experienced field archaeologist. She has excavated in the Andes for over ten years. However, Dr. Sharratt's work spans both archaeology and anthropology and constitutes a deeply reflective use of museum collections for teaching together with sensitive collaboration with museum scholars in both anthropology and conservation science. The interdisciplinary as well as inter-institutional character of Dr. Sharratt's work has enabled her to achieve such resonant results, taking her students—and now us—from an apparently modest article of textile craft to a complex and varied cosmology distributed among distinct but related societies in western South America over two millennia.

To pretend that Dr. Sharratt's project, *Carrying Coca*, is devoid of political implications would be disingenuous. The place of coca—its cultivation and consumption—in Andean societies is heavily contested, in large part owing to the appetite of the developed world for its refined derivative, cocaine. Its consumption in whatever form by people, whether rich or impoverished, in the wealthy North has had a huge impact on long-established lifeways in Andean regions, prompting sometimes violent responses to U.S.–sponsored punitive actions, such as crop eradication campaigns. Commentators frequently present the resurgent political organization of Indigenous peoples, exemplified by the election of Evo Morales to the presidency of Bolivia—he took office in 2006—as a self-protective backlash against neocolonial interference that, in effect, licenses drug consumption among the privileged elite of North America while victimizing Indigenous Andeans. To consume a line of coke is to threaten the security—even the very life—of an Andean agricultural worker. Coca is integral to the viability of economic, social, and cultural sustainability among some of the world's poorest and most marginalized communities. Nicola Sharratt's *Carrying Coca* is many things, among them a demonstration of long-sustained cultural values, human inventiveness within traditions, and imaginative adaptability in the face of colonialism and globalization. Yet it is also a reminder that outsiders who threaten the long-held values of Indigenous peoples—in this case, of many thousands of native Quechua and Aymara speakers—might do well to pause and reconsider the disruption, destruction, and misery their actions engender.

——Ivan Gaskell
    Professor of Cultural History and Museum Studies
    Curator and Head of the Focus Gallery Project
    Bard Graduate Center

Author's Acknowledgments

Many individuals and institutions made *Carrying Coca* possible. The exhibition and catalogue are the result of a collaborative relationship between the Bard Graduate Center (BGC) and the American Museum of Natural History (AMNH), and I thank the individuals who conceived of and facilitated this unique fellowship opportunity: Dean Peter Miller at the BGC and Charles Spencer, Laurel Kendall, and Dean John Flynn at the AMNH.

The Focus Gallery Project at the BGC provides a unique space for incorporating graduate students into every stage of curatorial practice, and student participation was central to the development of *Carrying Coca*. Corinne Brandt, Liz Donato, Maeve Hogan, Sarah Pickman, and Antonio Sánchez Gómez all contributed substantially through their research in the spring of 2013 on the coca bags selected for the exhibition. Equally as important were their lively contributions to class discussions in which we investigated *Carrying Coca*'s core themes. The digital interactive developed by MediaCombo grew out of the creative ideas and hard work of Brandt, Pickman, and Sánchez Gómez in the fall of 2013 under the expert guidance of Kimon Keramidas. Thanks also go to Kelsey Brow for her contributions throughout the process, especially during early research, and to Sophia Lufkin for diligently reading and editing label copy.

I owe a debt of gratitude to the many people at the BGC who, under Susan Weber's leadership, foster an institution that so successfully integrates research, teaching, and curatorial practice. Ivan Gaskell has been enormously supportive since I arrived at the BGC, responding to the initial idea for *Carrying Coca* with enthusiasm and challenging me to push the concept in new ways. It has been a delight to work with and learn from the BGC Gallery's staff, headed by Nina Stritzler-Levine. Ann Marguerite Tartsinis has been fundamental to the entire process, and I thank her for skillfully keeping this project on track. The talents of Kate DeWitt, Marianne Lamonaca, Alexis Mucha, Ian Sullivan, and Han Vu were all vital in making the exhibition and catalogue a reality. Thanks also to the staff of Academic Programs at the BGC— Jamie Cavallo, Keith Condon, Marc LeBlanc, and Elena Pinto Simon—especially for their work organizing a symposium related to *Carrying Coca*—and to Rebecca Allan for crafting a diverse array of public programs around the exhibition.

The AMNH has been my other institutional home during this fellowship. Charles Spencer has been encouraging and supportive throughout my time at the museum. I also especially thank Sumru Aricanli for warmly welcoming me into the South American lab. This project would not have been possible without the expert knowledge and skills that the AMNH staff brings to the collections. I am particularly indebted to Samantha Alderson, Tom Baione, Paul Beelitz, Anita Caltabiano, John Hansen, Barry Landua, Judith Leveson, Kristen Mable, Barbara Mathé, Mary Lou Murillo, Gregory Raml, Mai Reitmeyer, and Gabrielle Tieu.

Visits to other museums enabled me to broaden considerably the scope of the project. I thank the staff of those museums for taking the time to show me collections of coca bags, especially Nancy Rosoff at the Brooklyn Museum in New York, Helen Wolfe and Jago Cooper at the British Museum in London, and Patricia Palacios Filinich and Antonio Oquiche Hernani at the Museo Contisuyo in Moquegua, Peru. Through e-mail, Ann Rowe of the Textile Museum in Washington, D.C., generously advised on particularly confounding textiles that I encountered during the research stage of the project.

Thanks also to the Quechua Outreach Committee at the Center for Latin American and Caribbean Studies at New York University and the New York Quechua Initiative, whose members are raising the profile of Quechua–speaking communities in the New York City area and who were important partners in the development of *Carrying Coca*.

This catalogue benefited enormously from the constructive and encouraging comments of an anonymous reviewer, as well as feedback from and discussion with several other individuals: Sarah Baitzel, Abigail Balbale, Sofia Chacaltana Cortez, Ana Cristina Londoño, Marion O'Connor, Elizabeth Plunger, and Bernard Sharratt. Thanks to John Hicks for preparing the map. I especially thank Ivan Gaskell for reading multiple iterations of the catalogue, and for encouraging me to rethink the material in productive ways, and Barbara Burn for her skillful edits to the manuscript.

I sincerely thank Ryan Williams and Jonathan Haas for bringing me on as ethnographer for the Field Museum collections project "Ceramic and Textile Arts of the Descendants of the Incas." The fieldwork I conducted between 2007 and 2009 under the auspices of that project sparked my interest in the long history and social complexity of Andean textiles, and I drew on that fieldwork extensively during the development of *Carrying Coca*. Eloy Percy Lopez, Wilson Jaime Callañupa, and Raul Menaút Huacan provided invaluable logistical and translation assistance. The project was enhanced by the participation of students from the University of Illinois at Chicago in 2008 and 2009. I owe a huge debt of gratitude to the many individual weavers who shared their stories and explained techniques and designs. Special thanks go to Nilda Callañupa Alvarez, who generously invited me to spend six weeks with the Centro de Textiles Tradicionales del Cusco in 2007 and whose efforts to revitalize weaving in the Andes are without equal. I am also very grateful to Ysidora Yony Nina Jorge, Hermalinda Condori Centeno, and Carmen Jorge Flores, who made the research in highland Moquegua in 2008 and 2009 possible. Ysidora Yony Nina Jorge and Fermina Flores Ticona offered specific insight into coca bags during follow-up conversations in the summer of 2013.

Mike Dillon made me aware of the database of slides on coca held at the Field Museum and encouraged me to make use of the impressive visual record there. Baldomero Caceres Santa Maria generously welcomed me into his home in Lima in 2013 and shared a lifetime of research on coca. I also thank the *curanderos*, particularly Carmen Jorge Flores, Don Juan Lopez, and Rosa Choque, who allowed me to participate in numerous *pagos* over the past decade. They have shared their knowledge as ritual specialists and enabled me to witness firsthand the importance of coca in ceremonial practices in the Andes today and my experiences with them were integral to *Carrying Coca*'s development.

——Nicola Sharratt

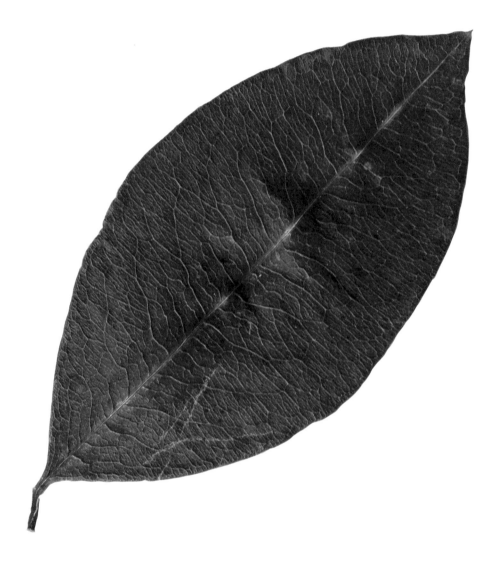

Fig. 1. Coca leaf. Purchased in Torata, Department of Moquegua, Peru, 2013.

Introduction

*No Indian is without his chuspa or coca-bag, made of llama-cloth, dyed red and blue in
patterns, with woolen tassels hanging from it. He carries it over one shoulder, suspended at his
side; and in taking coca, he sits down, puts his chuspa before him, and places the leaves in
his mouth one by one, chewing and turning them till he forms a ball.*

——Sir Clements Markham, *Travels in Peru and India* (1862)

For thousands of years the coca plant has held an essential and unparalleled place in the
daily activities, customs, and ritual practices of communities in the Andean region of
South America. People living in the Andes routinely chew coca leaves (fig. 1) to counter-
act the challenges of the extreme South American environment. A mild stimulant, coca
invigorates workers during arduous labor and, thanks to its many curative properties,
is a vital ingredient in medicinal preparations. Friends and relatives share its leaves in
myriad ways, and as such, coca symbolizes and mediates social relationships, entwin-
ing communities and individuals in ongoing bonds of reciprocity. Imbued with sacred
qualities, offerings of coca leaves nourish mother earth (*Pacha Mama*) and placate the
ever-present and unpredictable mountain gods (*apu*).

Such an important and ubiquitous substance demands its own dedicated container,
and for centuries people of the Andes have carried coca leaves in small woven bags. These
bags are called *chuspas* in Quechua, the most extensively spoken Andean language (fig. 2).[1]
Comparable in size and design to a purse and frequently equipped with a shoulder strap,
a *chuspa* has a specific purpose, but its construction of elaborate and exquisitely decorated
woven cloth indicates that it is not just a simple vessel (fig. 3).

Chuspas realize the physical and metaphorical intersection of textiles and coca
leaves. Both textiles and coca have deep-seated cultural and adaptive importance in
Andean South America. In addition to its vital functional value as a barrier against the
bitter cold that plagues the mountainous zones of the Andes, cloth is also a primary
artistic medium. Highland textiles are traditionally woven from the hair of native
camelids, usually the domesticated alpacas and llamas and, more rarely, wild vicuña and
guanaco. Renowned for their high quality, varied techniques, and elaborate designs,
Andean textiles are also important symbols of social identity. As part of this tradition,
chuspas constitute embodiments of specialist skills, expressions of artistic repertoires, and
displays of cultural affiliation.

However, as carriers of coca leaves, *chuspas* are much more than aesthetically pleas-
ing and technically sophisticated pieces of art. In their actual and symbolic connection
with coca, *chuspas* are embedded in the story of this sacred and contested substance.
They are objects that are used, interacted with, essential to cultural practice, and important in social relationships, ritual activity, and political negotiation.[2] In examining coca
leaves and the bags that hold them, this essay and the accompanying exhibition present
a story of tradition and transformation. How *chuspas* are made, what they look like, who
wears them, and when and how they are used result not only from variations in Andean
textile traditions but also from the ways in which coca is utilized and perceived both in
the Andes and beyond.

Beginning with a brief introduction to the geography and history of Andean South
America and to the region's weaving traditions, I then examine how coca bags in many respects represent a deeply resilient component of Andean craft production. Since the

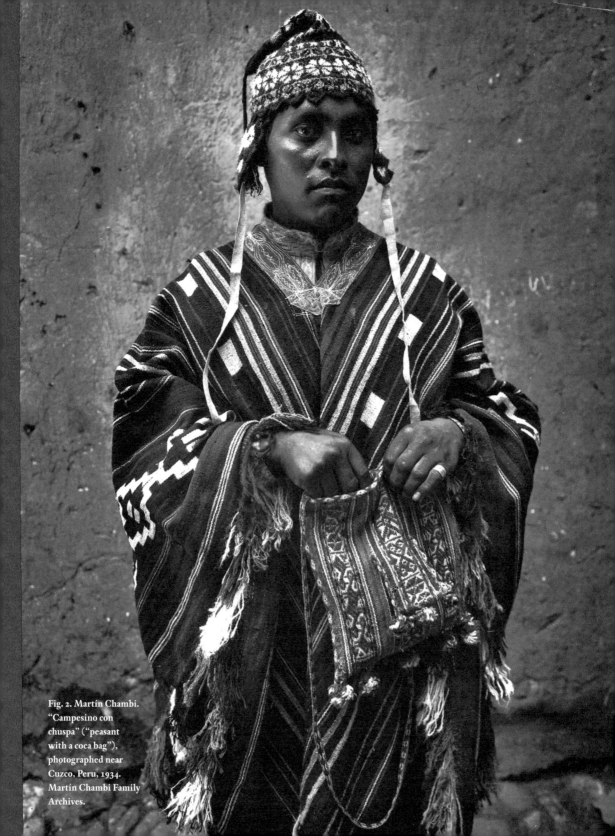

Fig. 2. Martín Chambi. "Campesino con chuspa" ("peasant with a coca bag"), photographed near Cuzco, Peru, 1934. Martín Chambi Family Archives.

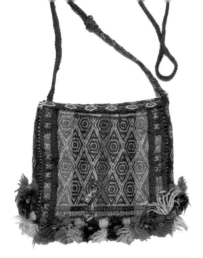

Fig. 3. Coca bag with strap. Collected in Pocoata, Bolivia, accessioned in 1969. Wool; double-faced warp pattern, braided strap. Courtesy of the Division of Anthropology, American Museum of Natural History, 40.1/3572. Cat. 29.

beginning of the first millennium AD, *chuspas* have been a constant presence in the archaeological, written, and visual record of the Andes. The general appearance of coca bags produced in highland communities in Peru and Bolivia in the twenty-first century is strikingly similar to those recovered from pre-Hispanic burials, yet in the details of their design and decoration, *chuspas* are testament to shifting fashions and technologies. Furthermore, as with other textiles in Andean South America, stylistic differences between contemporaneous *chuspas* distinguish them as the products of particular regions and communities.

However, *chuspas* are unique among Andean textiles because of the substance they hold, coca leaves. In examining coca's crucial role in the Andes, I suggest that there are consistencies in the ways *chuspas* have been integrated into Andean social networks and ritual practices. However, these consistencies belie the complexities in how *chuspas* are used and perceived, which are rooted in coca's historical trajectory. As I explore the ways in which this innocuous-looking plant has been embroiled in national and global politics for centuries, I highlight particular temporal periods during which *chuspas* underwent alterations in production, use, and perception.

After reviewing the complexities of coca bags within Andean society, I then turn to a current trend in which *chuspas* are created and used outside the communities of their traditional production. *Chuspas* are today part of a burgeoning trade for tourist souvenirs. At the same time, they are used less frequently in the traditional communities of their production and consumption, as those communities increasingly rely on expendable plastic bags instead of elaborately woven *chuspas*. The intertwined processes through which "traditional" handicrafts have become desirable global commodities and coca has been recast as a dangerous menace to be stamped out mean that after centuries of resilience in form, use, and cultural significance, *chuspas* have in just a few decades entered into a course of radical reinvention that potentially permanently alters how they are made, who wears them, and how they are used.

Throughout this essay I draw on a range of published sources and personally collected ethnographic information and refer to the earliest written records from South America, archaeological site reports, ethnographies of Andean life, and international agreements. The essay is informed by the direct examination of Andean collections housed in museums in Latin America, the United States, and Europe,[3] and in my discussions of both textiles and coca I have incorporated into this essay ethnographic data that I collected in Peru and Bolivia during the past decade.[4]

This essay accompanies the exhibition *Carrying Coca*, held at the Bard Graduate Center in New York in the spring of 2014. The exhibition displays *chuspas* and other objects from the permanent collections of the American Museum of Natural History (AMNH). In a short afterword, I review how these particular *chuspas* came to New York in order to illuminate the ways in which research methodologies a century ago have impacted the construction and development of this exhibition.

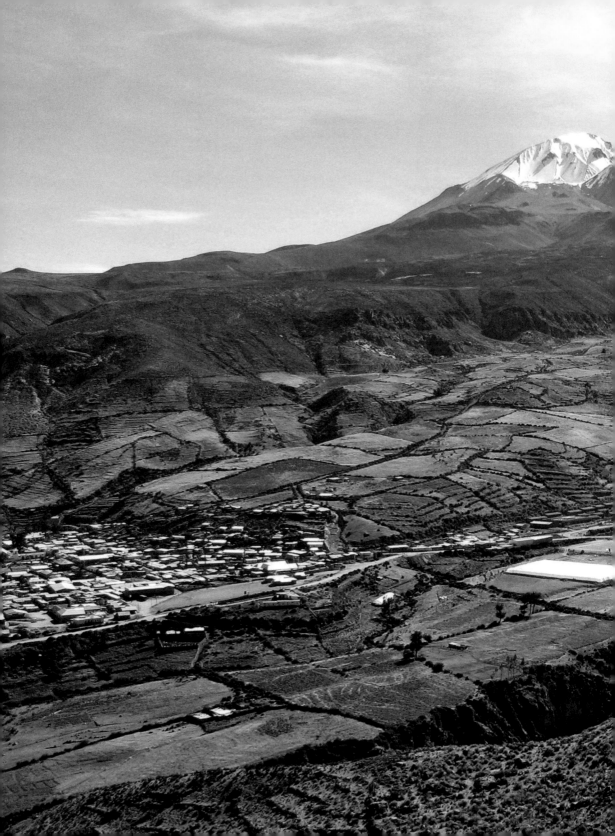

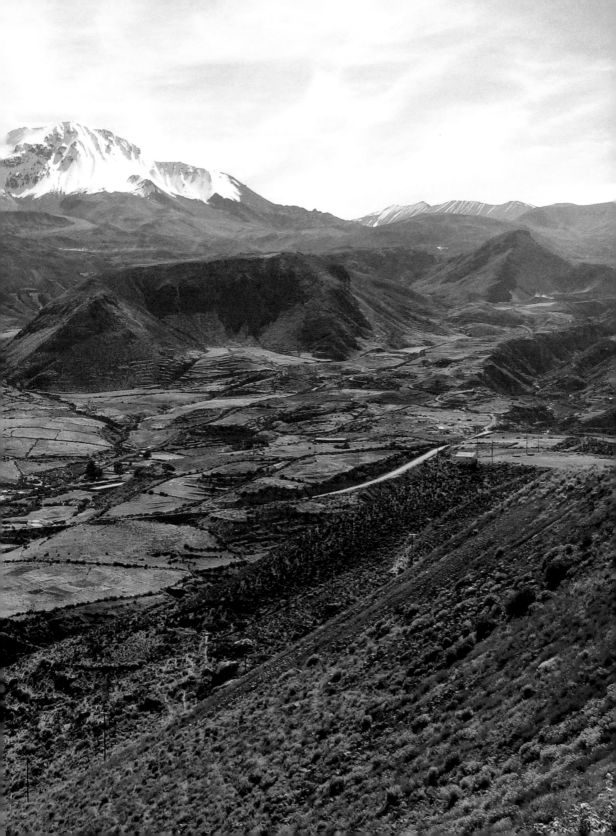

Fig. 4 (overleaf).
Mount Tacora,
northern Chile.
The Field Museum
Anthropology
Collections, CU-0002.

Fig. 5 (bottom).
Locations mentioned
in the text. John Hicks.

Fig. 6 (below).
Chronology of Andean
South America.

Early Pre-Ceramic
10,500 BC–6000 BC
Earliest human occupants

Middle Pre-Ceramic
6000–3000 BC
First villages in the Andes

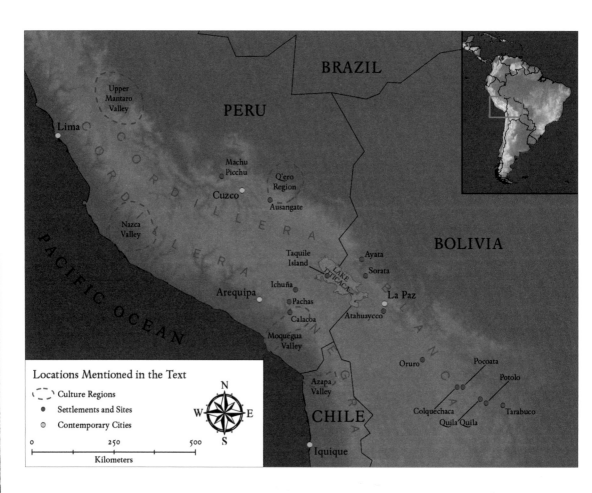

Locations Mentioned in the Text

- - - Culture Regions
● Settlements and Sites
◎ Contemporary Cities

0   250   500
Kilometers

Andean South America and Its Weaving Traditions

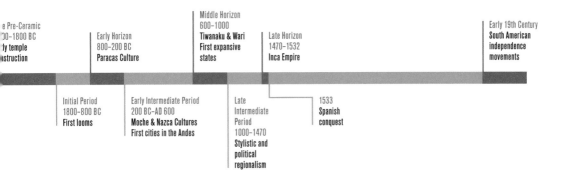

| e Pre-Ceramic
J0–1800 BC
ly temple
Istruction | | Early Horizon
800–200 BC
Paracas Culture | | Middle Horizon
600–1000
Tiwanaku & Wari
First expansive
states | Late Horizon
1470–1532
Inca Empire | | Early 19th Century
South American
independence
movements |

| | Initial Period
1800–800 BC
First looms | Early Intermediate Period
200 BC–AD 600
Moche & Nazca Cultures
First cities in the Andes | Late
Intermediate
Period
1000–1470
Stylistic and
political
regionalism | 1533
Spanish
conquest |

A region of breathtaking beauty and climatic extremes, Andean South America sprawls across half a continent, encompassing an incredible array of environmental zones. Two mountain ranges, the Cordillera Blanca and the Cordillera Negra, dominate and define the region. Formed by millennia of tectonic activity that buckled the terrain into jagged peaks, these snow-capped mountains stretch for 4,300 miles, their highest summits reaching almost 20,000 feet above sea level before tumbling into fertile highland valleys. To their west, one of the driest deserts in the world lies along the Pacific coast of Peru and Chile. To their east, semitropical slopes covered in dense vegetation are the gateway to the largest river system on earth, the Amazon Basin, and in a cold, windswept, and arid plain called the *altiplano*, the waters of Lake Titicaca glisten (figs. 4, 5, see fig. 8).

People have occupied these diverse and dramatic landscapes for at least 12,500 years. The earliest humans lived in small nomadic groups, surviving on wild plants and animals. Between 6000 and 3000 BC, people established the first villages along the arid coastal strip. Villagers exploited the rich marine resources of the Pacific Ocean and over time began to cultivate crops and domesticate small herds of native animals. By the middle of the third millennium BC, the descendants of these communities were constructing monumental temple complexes. From approximately AD 1, powerful leaders were ruling densely populated, socially stratified cities on the north coast of Peru. Beginning about AD 600, two expansive states, the Wari and Tiwanaku, dominated politics, economics, and ideology across the Andes and established an extensive network of colonies connected by trade and exchange. Their violent collapse about AD 1000 resulted in a fragmented and unstable social landscape in which diverse groups and artistic traditions developed, but by the fourteenth century, the Andes were again politically and culturally united when the Inca state began its rapid expansion from the Cuzco valley. Within a century, the Inca polity grew into the largest pre-Hispanic empire in the Americas with a population of six million and a territory stretching from modern Chile to Ecuador (fig. 6).[5]

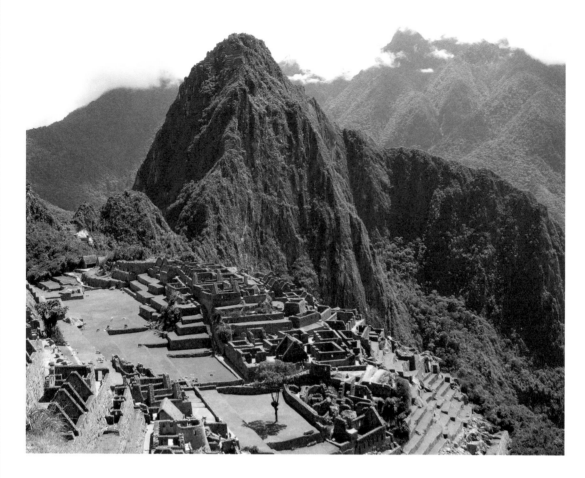

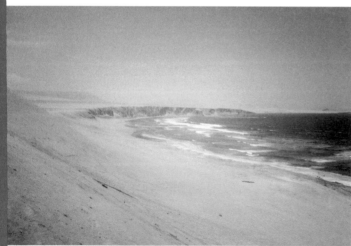

Fig. 7 (above). Inca
site of Machu Picchu,
Peru's principal tourist
destination, 2007.

Fig. 8 (left).
Pacific coast of
Peru, 2001.

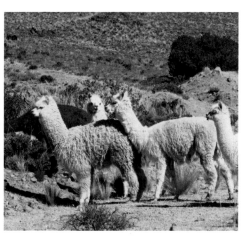

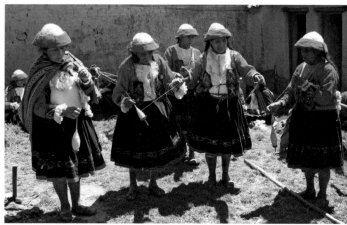

The Spanish conquest in 1533 brought this vast empire to a sudden end, and South America remained under European control until the nineteenth century, when a series of independence movements resulted in the creation of the nation-states that endure to the present day. The political violence that plagued several Andean countries in the second half of the twentieth century has been largely replaced by established democracies and strong, growing economies that compete on the global stage. In this era of security and stability, the region has opened up to an influx of visitors, and today tourism focused primarily on the Andes' rich and very visible archaeological heritage constitutes a vast and profitable industry (fig. 7).[6]

Andean Weaving Traditions

In an area of such dramatic environments, textiles produced with the hair of native camelids are essential cultural responses to the cold and wind that plagues the high-altitude regions of the Andes (fig. 9), whereas cooler fabrics made from the native cotton (*Gossypium barbadense*) that grows on the Pacific coast offer shade from the high-intensity sun in that area.[7] In this region, camelid fibers and cotton both exist in several natural colors ranging from cream to brown, and both fibers have been dyed with plants and minerals since pre-Hispanic times (see fig. 13).[8] Weavers continue to craft "traditional" Andean textiles using relatively simple and enduring technologies.[9] Textile artists spin

cotton, camelid fiber, and sheep's wool, introduced by the Spanish, using hand spindles with whorls made of ceramic, wood, and bone (fig. 10, see cat. 16), and they weave spun threads on a variety of loom types. The portable back-strap loom, which has changed little from pre-Hispanic predecessors, and horizontal four-stake ground looms are both used to weave large textiles, whereas smaller looms attached to a single stake or even the weaver's toe are used for weaving narrow pieces, such as belts and straps. Andean woven cloth is finished on all edges directly on the loom. When a weaver completes this four-selvage textile, she removes the parts of the loom from the cloth rather than cutting the threads, as in most other world cultures.

The origins of these traditions are almost as old as human occupation of the region, having begun some 12,000 years ago. The earliest identified textiles are mats made of plant fiber, which was beaten into filaments and interlaced by hand to create a structure.[10] The first decorated textiles were recovered from archaeological contexts dating to 3000–1800 BC, pre-dating the creation of the loom, and their designs consist of repetitive zoomorphic images, including serpents, condors, and crabs.[11] Pre-Hispanic weavers first constructed and used looms about 1400 BC. Major innovations in embroidery, tapestry, painted textiles, and tie-dye followed and would form the basis for some of the most famous pre-Hispanic textiles, those created by the coastal Paracas and Nazca cultures in

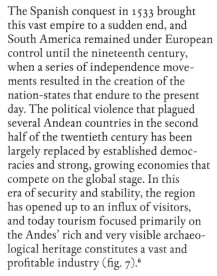

Fig. 9 (left). Alpacas in Carumas, Peru, 2013.

Fig. 10 (right). Women spinning in Patabamba, Department of Cuzco, Peru, 2007. The Field Museum Anthropology Collections, CU-0002.

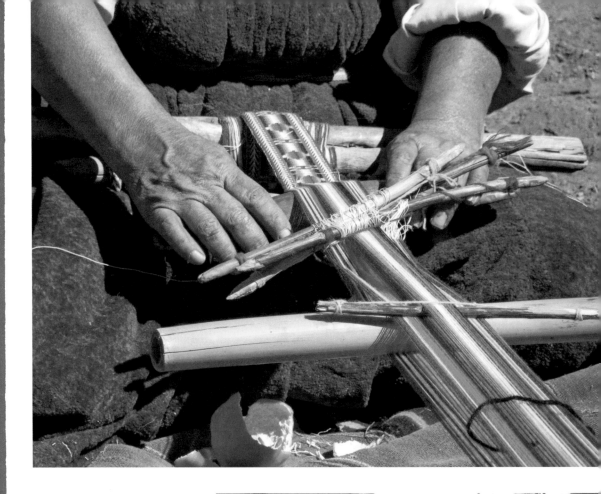

Fig. 11 (above). Weaving a belt from synthetic fibers, San Cristobal, Department of Moquegua, Peru, 2008. The Field Museum Anthropology Collections, CU-0002.

Fig. 12 (right). Tourist market in Arequipa, Peru, 2013.

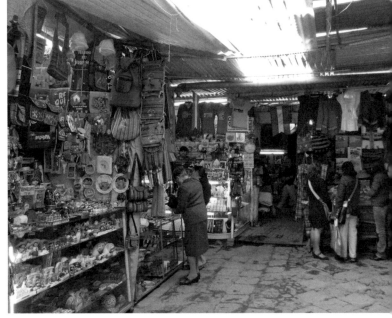

the centuries around the turn of the first millennium.[12] The later Tiwanaku and Wari states are known for tapestry weavings that materialized state ideologies in their woven depictions of political and supernatural motifs.[13]

During the Inca period, textiles constituted a socially and economically important good. Demanded as tribute from every household within the empire, offered in sacrifices,[14] and proffered as gifts to cement political relationships and reward loyalty to the state, Inca cloth was graded by quality.[15] The finest tapestry-woven fabric, called *cumbi,* was restricted to the highest social ranks, and specialist weavers produced *cumbi* cloth under the direct sponsorship of the ruling elite. One group of specialists known as *aqllakuna* was selected from the most beautiful girls in the empire and sequestered in special compounds to weave fine cloth for the state until they were given as wives to noblemen.[16]

The Spanish conquest introduced foreign technologies, including the spinning wheel and the treadle loom, and materials such as sheep's wool and silk.[17] The conquerors both co-opted Inca systems of textile production and put native weavers to work in Spanish workshops. Even when Andean weavers continued to use pre-Hispanic-style looms and native fibers, the types of textiles they wove were altered by European decorative repertoires and concepts of modest dress. The skirts (*polleras*) and pants that constitute fundamental components of highland Andean dress today were garment forms adapted after the Spanish conquest and contrast with the woven wrapped dresses and tunics produced and worn by the Incas.[18]

The importance of textiles in Andean communities continues to the present day. As in pre-Hispanic times, textiles still play a fundamental role in communicating social identities. In the Andean highlands, dress demarcates ethnic identity, village membership, gender, and age.[19] However, the incorporation of synthetic fibers, chemically based dyes, and machine-made cloth has changed the types of textiles produced and the exact methods of production used in the past century. Weavers purchase synthetic fibers that are already spun and thus save a considerable amount of labor and time. Simultaneously, the foreign demand for alpaca wool has restricted access to traditional fibers within some Andean communities.[20] The shift from natural to synthetic fibers has altered not only the texture of woven fabrics but also their visual effect, by providing a much wider and brighter color palette (fig. 11).[21]

The explosion in Andean tourism today has created a flourishing souvenir trade. Portable and packable, textiles are ubiquitous in tourist markets, particularly in major destinations such as Cuzco, Arequipa, and La Paz (fig. 12).[22] Despite the changes in materials, designs, and motifs that Andean textiles have undergone through the centuries, sellers frequently market souvenir textiles as "Incan" and as evidence of unaltered Andean practice, conflating Andean history and indigenous customs on a grand scale. Weaving cooperatives, which not only craft products but also open their doors to visitors, are increasingly common in larger cities. Buying Andean textiles and experiencing, even participating in, their creation are now common and expected components of a vacation in the Andes.

Thus, textiles are woven into the very story of Andean South America. Initially a necessary strategic response to the environment, Andean weaving developed into an elaborate art form. Beyond their functional and aesthetic value, textiles have been affected by and integral to economics, politics, and ritual practice in Andean communities for millennia. *Chuspas* are an enduring element of this story and constitute one of the most resilient and consistently present woven forms in the history of Andean textile arts.

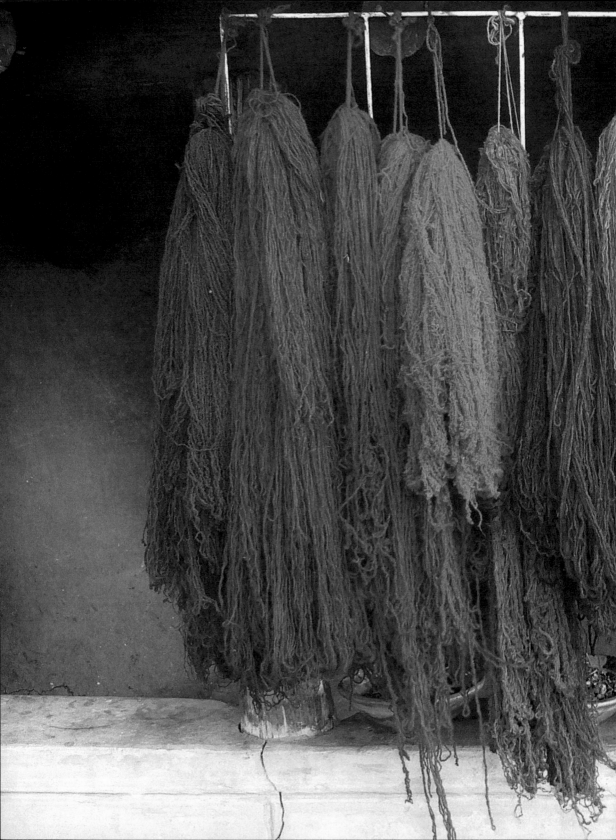

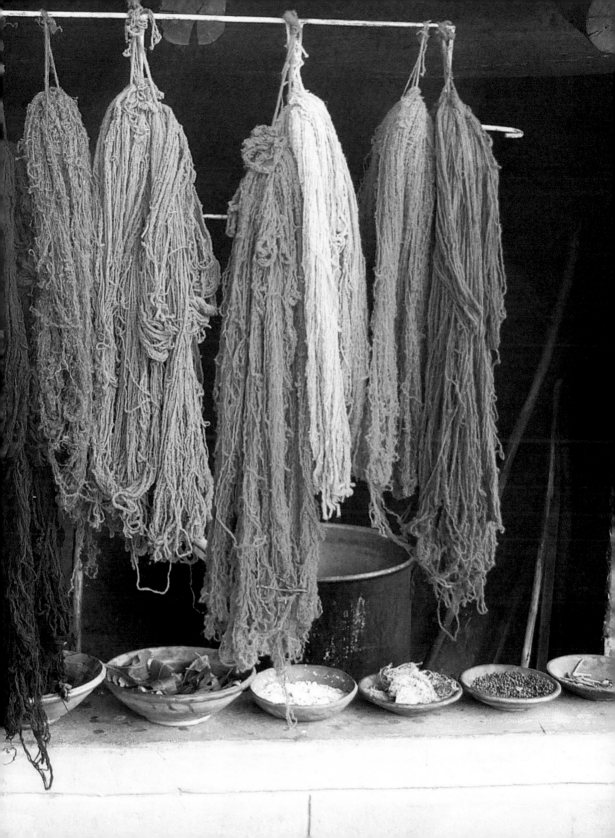

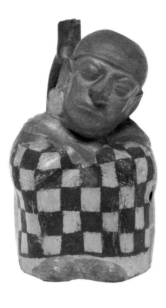

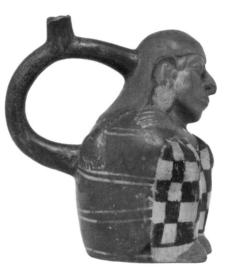

Fig. 13 (overleaf).
Wool colored with
mineral- and
plant-based dyes.
The Field Museum
Anthropology
Collections, CU-0002.

Fig. 14 (left). Two
views of stirrup-spout
vessel depicting elite
male asleep with
chuspa slung over his
shoulder. Moche, Peru,
AD 1–700. Molded
ceramic. Museum
of Archaeology
and Anthropology,
Cambridge University,
CUMAA 1924.190.

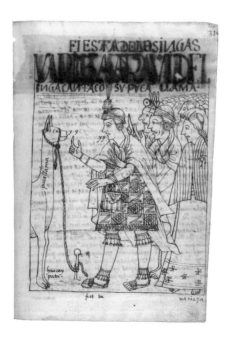

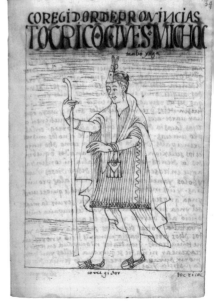

Chuspas

Figs. 15–18 (left to right). Felipe Guaman Poma de Ayala. "Fiesta of the Incas: The Inca sings with his red llama," page 320, drawing 124; "Governor of the Provinces," page 348, drawing 136; "Native horticulturalists tending their garden: 'Chew this coca, sister,'" page 879, drawing 324; "The First Captain, Inka Ypanqui," page 145, drawing 51; all from *El primer nueva corónica y buen gobierno*, 1615–16. Det Kongelige Bibliotek, Copenhagen, Denmark.

27

Chuspas

Depictions and Descriptions

Long before the Spanish arrived in Peru, Andean artists portrayed people wearing *chuspas.* Most surviving images of *chuspas* are on pottery vessels, thanks to the preferential preservation of ceramic in the archaeological record.[23] Between AD 1 and 700, the Moche dominated the north coast of Peru, and during that time Moche ceramic artists produced startlingly lifelike representations of people, plants, and animals in molded ceramic vessels. A ceramic vessel in the Museum of Archaeology and Anthropology at the University of Cambridge shows an elite male curled up asleep with a *chuspa* slung over his shoulder (fig. 14).[24]

Depictions of *chuspas* in multiple media since pre-Hispanic times testify to the endurance of this form. *Chuspas* are particularly notable in the seventeenth-century line drawings that accompany Felipe Guaman Poma de Ayala's lengthy description of Inca customs. Although he rarely emphasizes them in his text, he illustrates *chuspas* in at least seventeen separate drawings, associated with a range of individuals, including Inca kings and queens, local political leaders, and healers (figs. 15, 16). Guaman Poma includes *chuspas* in an extensive variety of contexts, as two individuals share coca

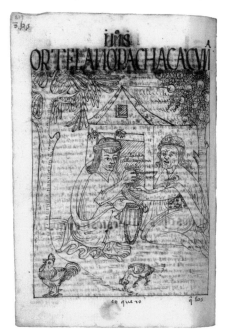

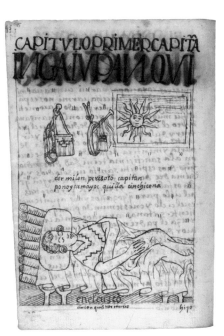

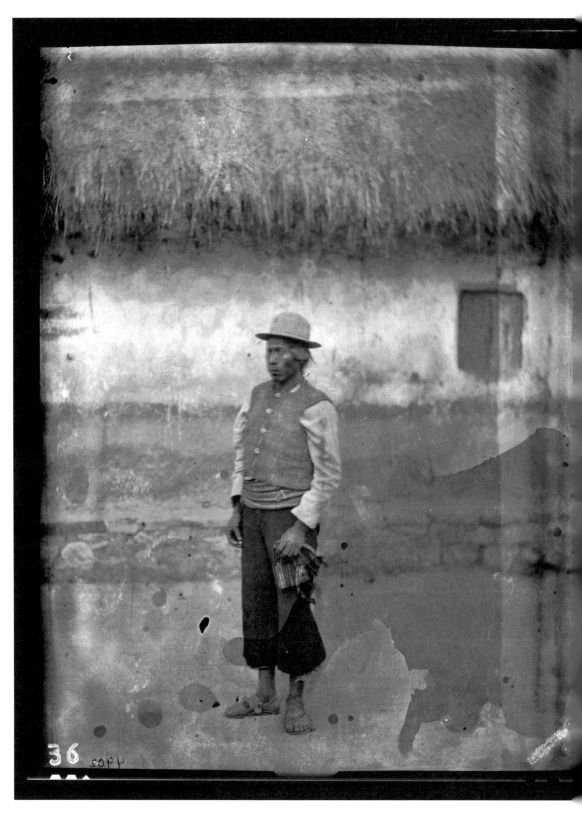

36 copy

during horticulture, in ritual settings, at funerals, in festivals, and in parades (fig. 17). In one drawing he shows a *chuspa* hanging on a wall where its owner had left it before going to sleep (fig. 18).[25] Some of the earliest nineteenth-century photographs of Andean dress (fig. 19) also show people wearing coca bags, and they are common in twentieth-century ethnographic images as well.

Written descriptions of Andean *chuspas,* or *huallqepos* as they are called in Aymara, another widely spoken Andean language, are also remarkably consistent from the Spanish conquest to the present.[26] In 1609 Bernabe Cobo wrote that underneath his mantle and over his tunic a man would carry "a small *chuspa* which hangs around the neck. It is more or less one span in length and about the same width. This bag hangs down by the waist under the right arm, and the strap from which it hangs passes over the left shoulder."[27]

More than two and a half centuries later, following a trip to South America, the explorer and geographer Sir Clements Markham made the assertion that opens this essay: "No Indian is without his *chuspa* or coca-bag, made of llama-cloth, dyed red and blue in patterns, with woolen tassels hanging from it. He carries it over one shoulder, suspended at his side; and in taking coca, he sits down, puts his *chuspa* before him, and places the leaves in his mouth one at a time, chewing and turning them till he forms a ball."[28]

Nearly 150 years after Markham, in 2003, Andrea Heckman noted that in Ausangate, Peru, "men are rarely without their *chuspas*, which are often finely woven and often have a separate supplemental pocket for *llipta*, the lime ash catalysts that activates the alkaloids in coca."[29]

These visual representations and written descriptions demonstrate the ubiquity of *chuspas* and suggest that coca bags are relatively straightforward and conservative items, but in fact variations are evident in the actual objects that have survived. Through time, Andean *chuspas* have differed in technique and design, which distinguish them as prod-

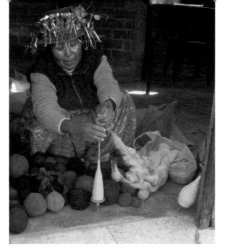

Fig. 19 (opposite). Adolph Bandelier, *Alcalde* (mayor) of Challa, holding a coca bag, photographed 1892—1903. Image 44336, American Museum of Natural History Library.

Fig. 20 (left). Spinning fiber. Department of Moquegua, Peru, 2008. The Field Museum Anthropology Collections, CU-0002.

ucts for specific peoples and uses. When situated geographically, temporally, and socially, *chuspas* are revealed to be complex objects whose trajectory in the Andes is embedded in the dual stories of textiles and coca.

Surviving archaeological examples of *chuspas* reveal a great deal about the technological and artistic repertoires evident in the Andes at different periods. Ethnographic *chuspas* are testament to the many forms and designs that coexisted across the Andes at the same time. However, *chuspas* do more than reflect. They also send messages about their wearers, such as gender, age, status, community, and ethnicity. Further, by carrying by carrying the coca leaves that are central to social relationships and spiritual engagement, *chuspas* directly contribute to cultural practice in the Andes.

Crafting *Chuspas*

The *chuspas* seen by Cobo, Markham, and Heckman were all made with similar tools and techniques, like those used for producing larger items, such as shawls and ponchos. Although the technologies are relatively simple, their use demands a considerable investment in time and labor. For example, it can take well over a week to make a *chuspa*, a comparatively small object.

The crafting process incorporates three basic stages: spinning, weaving, and embellishing. Using a hand spindle, a weaver spins cotton, camelid fiber, or sheep's wool into a thread (fig. 20) and

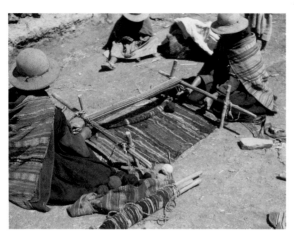
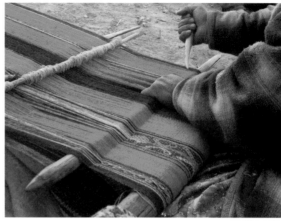

then twists or plies two or more spun threads together to strengthen the yarn.[30] When she has spun and plied enough yarn,[31] the weaver turns to her loom. Horizontal ground looms are particularly common in the southern Andes, where most of the *chuspas* in this essay were made.[32] Once the weaver has warped the loom by continuously wrapping a length of yarn in a figure-eight around the bars at each end of the loom (fig. 21),[33] she can begin to interlace the weft threads into the warp to create a structure (fig. 22).[34] Although plain weave is the simplest and most common structure in Andean weaving,[35] and is typically warp-faced,[36] weavers use a range of more complex weaving techniques in order to achieve the elaborate designs seen in *chuspas* and other Andean cloth. These include, but are not limited to, tapestry (fig. 23), in which weft threads in a range of colors are used to create motifs;[37] supplementary warp and weft techniques, which create designs by floating additional warps or wefts over the plain weave background; and complementary warp weaves, which involve at least two sets of warp threads in different colors. This last technique is particularly common in highland Andean textiles, such as the coca bag from the Island of Taquile (fig. 24).[38]

Regardless of the technique utilized, after the weaver is finished, she removes the loom pieces and is left with a four-selvage length of cloth, which is folded in half and stitched along the sides to create the basic bag shape of a *chuspa*. Although simple stitching is seen in some coca bags, weavers often create a tubular edging to ensure that the sides are more securely held together. This is achieved by executing either a cross-knit loop stitch or hand-woven edge bindings (fig. 25).[39] In the case of the latter, a weaver sews the binding onto the cloth as she weaves it.[40] When the body of the bag has been completed, the weaver adds straps, which can be simple cords or braided yarn. If woven, straps are made separately from the bag, often in a simple warp-faced plain weave with warp stripes.[41] To finish, the weaver sews on tassels, fringes, beads, and other decorative additions according to local custom and her own aesthetic choices.

The hand-crafted *chuspas* that illustrate this essay, both archaeological and ethnographic pieces, were all produced using this process of spinning, weaving, and embellishing, and thus they constitute a recognizable class of object. Yet the technique and design of individual bags distinguish them as products of particular periods in the long history of Andean weaving.

Diversity through Time
The earliest textiles identified by scholars as coca bags appear well into the history of Andean weaving.[42] Excavators report finding *chuspas* in burial contexts from the Nazca Valley in the south of Peru and the Azapa Valley in northern Chile dating to the beginning of the first millennium AD, and they appear consistently in the archaeological record

Fig. 21 (left). Grace Goodell. Warping a four-stake horizontal ground loom in Bolivia, 1968. Courtesy of the Division of Anthropology, American Museum of Natural History.

Fig. 22 (right). Beating the weft into position with pick carved from a camelid bone. Department of Moquegua, Peru, 2008. The Field Museum Anthropology Collections, CU-0002.

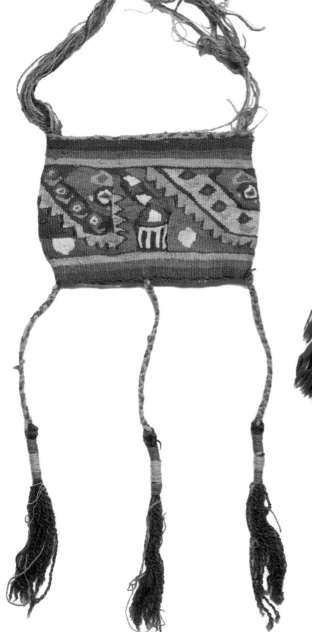

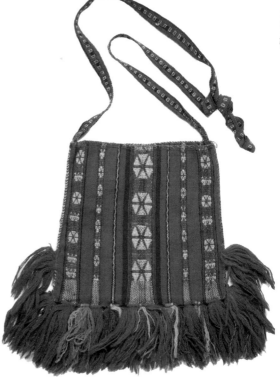

Fig. 23 (left). Bag. Central Coast, Peru, 1100–1532. Camelid fiber, cotton; weft-faced plain weave, slit tapestry, running overcasting stitches, and braiding. Courtesy of the Division of Anthropology, American Museum of Natural History, 41.2/7683. Cat. 24.

Fig. 24 (above). Bag with carrying strap, decorated with six-triangle motif that represents the social divisions of the community. Island of Taquile, Peru, accessioned in 1955. Wool; warp-faced plain weave, complementary warp-weave warp-patterned strap; edge binding of two-strand twining. Courtesy of the Division of Anthropology, American Museum of Natural History, 40.0/8870. Cat. 26.

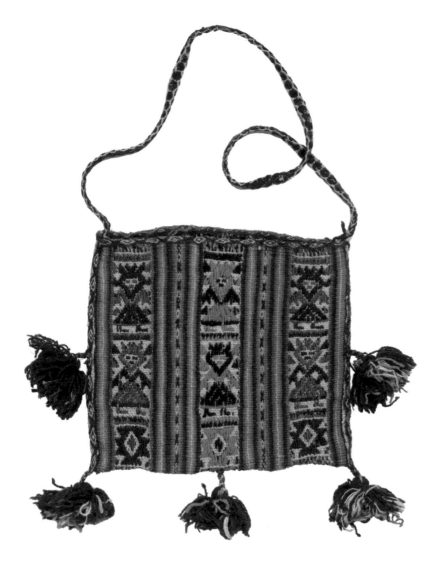

Fig. 25. Coca bag with
strap and hand-woven
edge bindings. Ayata,
Bolivia, accessioned
in 1969. Wool; single-
faced warp-patterned
stripes, plain weave
stripes, single-faced
warp-patterned
strap. Courtesy
of the Division
of Anthropology,
American Museum
of Natural History,
40.1/3582. Cat. 3.

Fig. 26 (opposite,
above). Two bags tied
together. Nazca Valley,
Peru, 100 BC–AD 700.
Camelid fiber, cotton;
double-faced tapestry
with eccentric wefts,
plied and beaded
fringes, braided strap.
Courtesy of
the Division of
Anthropology,
American Museum
of Natural History,
41.0/5461. Cat. 8.

Fig. 27 (opposite,
below). Bag. Nazca/
Wari, southern Peru,
AD 200–1000. Camelid
fiber; warp-faced
plain weave with
embroidery. Brooklyn
Museum, Gift of
George D. Pratt,
30.1215.

thereafter.[43] An exhaustive review of *chuspas* from all pre-Hispanic contexts is beyond the scope of this short essay, but a few specific examples highlight differences in *chuspa* fashions through time.[44]

Two Nazca bags (fig. 26) in the American Museum of Natural History are woven with camelid fiber and cotton in double-faced tapestry using eccentric wefts, with added plied and beaded fringes and braided straps. The Nazca were a confederacy of chiefdoms that occupied several valleys along the south coast of Peru between 100 BC and AD 700. Although evidence regarding provenance and a secure date is missing for the bags in figure 26, they likely date to the early Nazca period, as revealed by their zoomorphic iconography that probably depicts snakes. Early Nazca textile artists built on the artistic traditions of the earlier Paracas style by weaving images heavy with naturalistic designs and animal motifs.[45]

Another Nazca bag (fig. 27), now in the Brooklyn Museum, is woven in an entirely different manner, a warp-faced plain weave using only camelid fiber, and decorated with embroidery. This bag, although reminiscent in some respects of the Nazca bags in figure 26, has a slightly later date and is identified as Nazca/Wari.[46] In the seventh century, the region was conquered by the Wari state, which expanded from the capital in the Ayacucho Basin in the central highlands of Peru. Late Nazca textiles, such as this bag, show the influence of Wari styles in its increased use of camelid fiber and in the abstract, geometric motifs.

Roughly contemporaneous with the Nazca, the Moche state thrived on the north coast of Peru from AD 1 to 700. Textile evidence is more limited and fragmentary than for the Nazca.[47] Where they do survive, Moche textiles made with combinations of cotton and camelid fibers are not uncommon, with cotton used to create the structure of the textiles and camelid fiber for the supplementary warps and wefts. A bag in the South American collections at the Metropolitan Museum of Art is identified by museum staff as a coca bag (fig. 28). Woven in a camelid-fiber slit

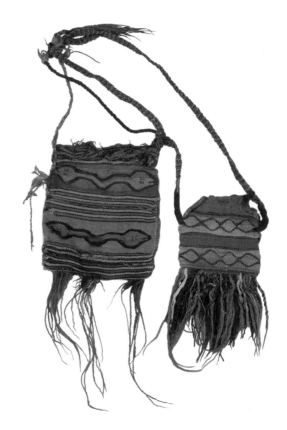

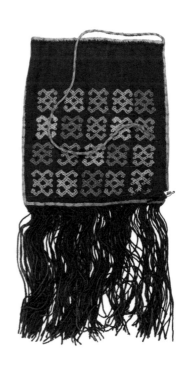

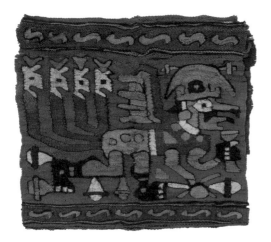

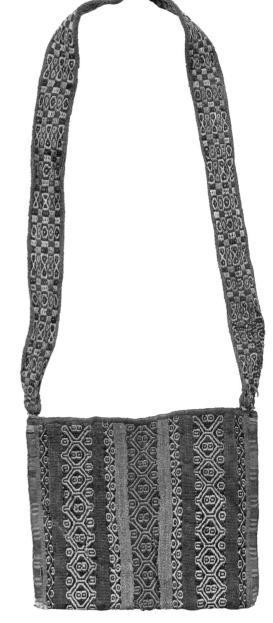

Fig. 28 (above). Coca bag. Moche, Peru, 5th–7th century. Camelid fiber, cotton; slit tapestry weave. The Metropolitan Museum of Art, Purchase, Bequest of Arthur M. Bullowa, 1993 (1994.35.88).

Fig. 29 (right). *Chuspa.* Inca, Peru, 1400–1533. Camelid fiber; vertical stripes of warp-faced plain weave alternating with patterned stripes of complementary weave; long handle attached. The Trustees of the British Museum, Am1921,0321.12.

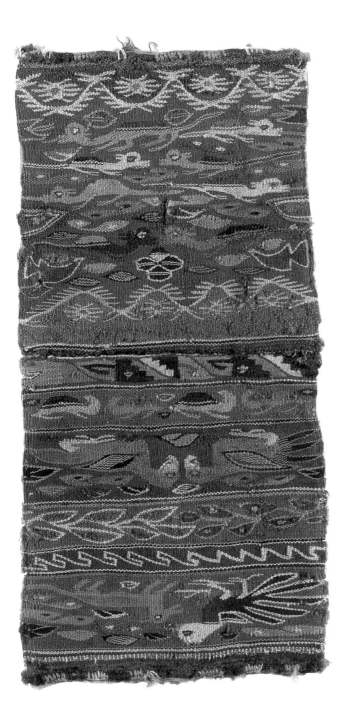

Fig. 30 (left). Colonial–
style *chuspa*. Cuzco,
Peru, late 16th–17th
century. Camelid
fiber; eccentric-weft
tapestry weave. The
Fine Arts Museums of
San Francisco, Jeffrey
Appleby Andean
Textile Collection,
L96.120.3.

Fig. 31 (below). Coca
bag. Probably Peru,
1532–1650. Camelid
fiber, cotton; slit
tapestry weave with
bands of two-color
complementary weft
plain weave with three-
span floats, joined
with fiber (camelid)
in cross-knit loop and
overcast stitches.
The Art Institute
of Chicago, Kate
S. Buckingham
Endowment,
1955.1830.

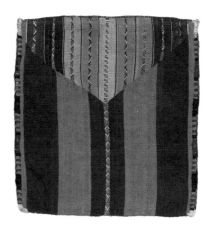

tapestry over a cotton warp, the bag is striking for its iconography. The figure suspended in the air is recognizable as an individual found in a scene called the Presentation Theme, which is found on numerous Moche ceramic vessels. The figure appears to be part human and part bird, with feathers and a beaklike nose. He wears a conical helmet and hands a goblet to the principal figure in the scene, which includes other elaborately dressed individuals and tortured prisoners. Some of these figures likely represent positions of authority at the pinnacle of Moche society,[48] and their depiction in portable media was an important means of disseminating images that legitimized state ideology and the religious and political authority of Moche leaders.[49]

A vast array of artistic traditions is apparent in the enormous cultural diversity present throughout the Andes during the centuries immediately before the emergence of the Inca state. Numerous regional styles are evident in museum-held chuspas that date to the time period AD 1000–1400, revealing completely different construction, technique, material, and iconography. The Chancay bag (see cat. 10) from the central coast of Peru is woven with camelid fiber in complementary-weft patterning to create an interlocking and repeating image. Its maker added embroidery, as well as a braided strap and plied fringe tassels. During this same period, weavers created a very different style using figurative and abstract designs in regions along the north coast of Chile pertaining to the Arica culture. Bags woven by this group often have a trapezoidal shape with a short cord for hanging them and are decorated with three bands illustrated with figurative and abstract designs.[50]

During the fourteenth and fifteenth centuries, as the Inca state spread thousands of miles across the Andes, people throughout the immense empire adopted Inca–style chuspas. To some degree, shared stylistic repertoires replaced the diversity of the previous centuries. Figure 29 is an exquisite example of a camelid fiber Inca chuspa in the British Museum. Made of one piece, folded in half with elaborate edge bindings, this

typical Inca chuspa has a woven strap[51] and is decorated with geometric motifs, particularly concentric hexagons seen in other Inca textile forms.

Colonial Period chuspas are materializations of the processes of culture contact that occurred in the wake of the 1533 Spanish conquest of the Andes. Extant examples of sixteenth- and seventeenth-century coca bags reveal syntheses of Andean and European concepts, techniques, and icons. A chuspa of this period from the Cuzco region (fig. 30), now in the Fine Arts Museum of San Francisco, is in many respects an exemplar of Andean workmanship. Constructed in weft-interlocked tapestry as a single complete web (here displayed open with the side stitching removed) and made with brilliantly dyed camelid fiber, the chuspa's imagery is radically different from the classic Inca style. The bag is decorated with images of feathered birds, abstract flowers, and animals that reveal clear European influences. Compared with articles of dress, the chuspa form changed little during the Colonial Period.[52] There are, however, rare examples of Colonial Period bags that show European–inspired modifications to their form, such as the example in figure 31, which also dates to the late sixteenth or early seventeenth century. Housed at the Art Institute of Chicago, this unusual bag is woven with alpaca fiber and is exquisitely executed in a tapestry weave.[53] Since the decoration includes stripes seen in Inca chuspas, the bag appears less obviously impacted by Spanish influences than the elaborate tapestry in figure 30, but instead of being left open at the top as with Inca and pre-Inca chuspas, this bag has a flap to close it, a style suggestive of European purses.

New ideas, technologies, and fibers introduced during the past two centuries have further impacted Andean weaving traditions and chuspa construction. One notable example is the tasseled coca bag (see cat. 25). Made of leather, a material not seen in pre-Hispanic or Colonial Period bags, it appears similar to others reported from the nineteenth century and later.[54] A new style of knitted bags is evident from the mid-twentieth century on, and some have entered ethnographic

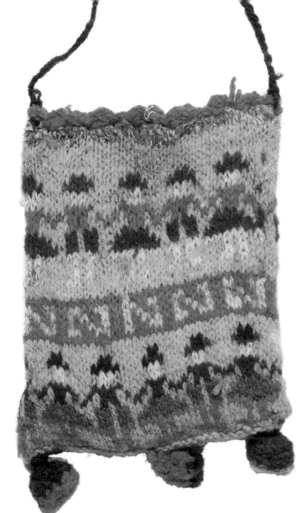

Fig. 32 (left). Bag
with coca leaves.
Peru, 1984. Wool;
knitted. Courtesy
of the Division
of Anthropology,
American Museum
of Natural History,
40.1/5036.

Fig. 33 (below).
Coca bag (*huallqepo*).
Calacoa, Department of
Moquegua, Peru, 2009.
Synthetic fibers; warp-
faced weave. Private
collection.

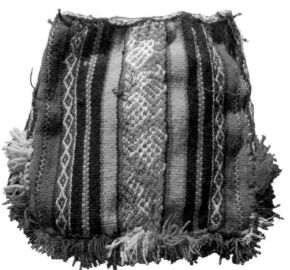

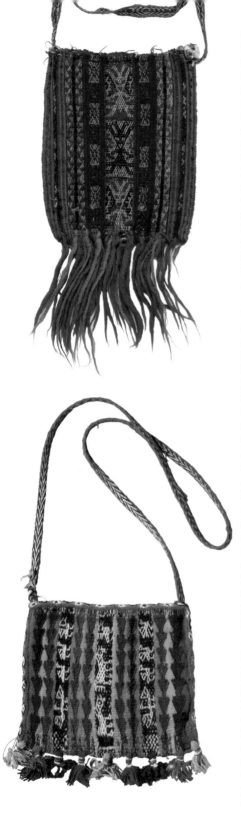

collections with coca leaves still inside (fig. 32). By the middle of the nineteenth century, synthetic colors gradually began to replace natural dyes, and synthetic fibers entered the weaving repertoire during the twentieth century. Inevitably, these fibers and dyes have further altered the feel and colors of *chuspas*, even where form and motifs are traditional (fig. 33). Construction details have also changed. Inca and pre-Inca bags are noted for their elaborate hand-woven edge bindings, which some twenty-first-century weavers assert is the only secure way to finish a bag and will devote two days to executing this technique. However, machine stitching is increasingly used instead, particularly in bags produced for the growing tourist industry.[55]

Andean weavers continue to craft traditional textiles, and coca bags are still used in communities throughout the Andes. In some villages, woven shawls and belts have changed rapidly in fashion, but coca bags appear to be guided by more conservative values and tastes. Although weavers incorporate new motifs, such as helicopters, swans, and the shield of Peru, into constantly changing design styles throughout Andean communities, coca bags often retain ancient motifs. Weavers in the Moquegua Valley of Peru, where coca bags are still commonly made and worn during fiestas, claim that *chuspas* are a more traditional garment type than other textile forms, and they produce coca bags decorated with the same set of designs as used on those produced fifty years ago. Although woven with synthetic fibers, the coca bag in figure 33 incorporates the same motifs used by generations of weavers in the region.[56]

Diversity in Space

Just as a chronological overview highlights the substantial changes the *chuspa* has undergone in the last 1,500 years, a brief comparison of twentieth-century coca bags from geographically distant locations across the Andes reveals the aesthetic range of this unique form. For example, the red coca bag in figure 34 was woven in Q'ero, a village in the Department of Cuzco, and decorated with motifs common in Cuzco: *ch'unchu*

Fig. 34 (above). Coca bag. Q'ero Village, Department of Cuzco, Peru, accessioned in 1956. Vicuña fiber; central warp-patterned stripe, warp stripe at selvage, fringed. Courtesy of the Division of Anthropology, American Museum of Natural History, 40.0/8906. Cat. 23.

Fig. 35 (below). Coca bag. Ichuña, Department of Moquegua, Peru, 2013. Synthetic fiber; warp-faced. Private collection.

(a dancer from the jungle), *inti* (a sun), and *qocha* (a lake). Although weavers frequently include these motifs in textiles produced throughout the region, their composition in vertical stripes makes this bag identifiable as a Q'ero piece.[57] By comparison, the vertically striped red bag from the Island of Taquile (see fig. 24), from the Peruvian side of Lake Titicaca, bears a six-triangle motif, which is very common in Taquilean weavings; weavers from the island report that it represents the division of the community into six social units (*suyus*).[58] Although coca bags have a common function, the icons used to decorate them have very particular associations and locally embedded meanings.

Two different bags (fig. 35, see fig. 33) from the same region, the Department of Moquegua in southern Peru, are more similar to one another than to the bags from Q'ero or Taquile. However, they exemplify the degree to which subtleties of design and construction differ, even in neighboring communities. Bags from the village of Calacoa, an Aymara–speaking community, and from the Quechua–speaking community of Ichuña, which is located within a few hours' walk, are similar in many ways, which suggests they are from the same region, but other features reveal exactly where they were produced. Calacoa coca bags (*huallqepos*) have a distinct design structure: a central decorative panel with figurative images and a narrower geometric stripe on each side. These bags are double-faced, and their straps are constructed of store-bought strips of cloth.[59] By contrast, Ichuña coca bags (*chuspas*) are single-faced and have woven straps. Their design structure that consists of three stripes of figurative motifs is a feature utilized in other woven accessories from the region. Figure 36 is a slightly larger strapless bag from another Quechua–speaking community, Pachas. Although not used for coca leaves, the bag incorporates the same decorative structure peculiar to the Quechua–speaking communities in this region and is therefore distinguished from its counterparts in nearby Aymara communities. Differences in textile designs have long acted as markers of identity. It takes specialized knowledge to recognize these very local and subtle differences, and these accessories serve as a means by which people within regions, even within a single valley, can distinguish themselves from others.

As we have seen, *chuspas* reflect the history of textile arts in Andean South America, but it is the sacred substance they carry, coca leaves, that differentiates them from other textiles and determines how they are constructed and used by their wearers. I turn now to the cultural importance and history of coca in the Andes as an integral part of cultural life and then explore how changing perceptions of coca in the Andes and beyond have affected who wears *chuspas*, how they are made, and the ways in which they are used and regarded.

Fig. 36. Gladys Ramos Ramos. *Canera*. Pachas, Department of Moquegua, Peru. Accessioned in 2008. Synthetic fibers. The Field Museum, A115022d_004.

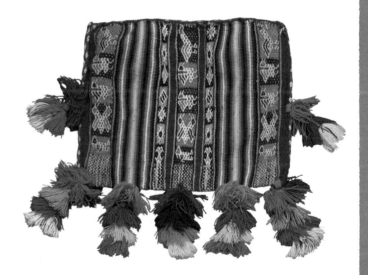

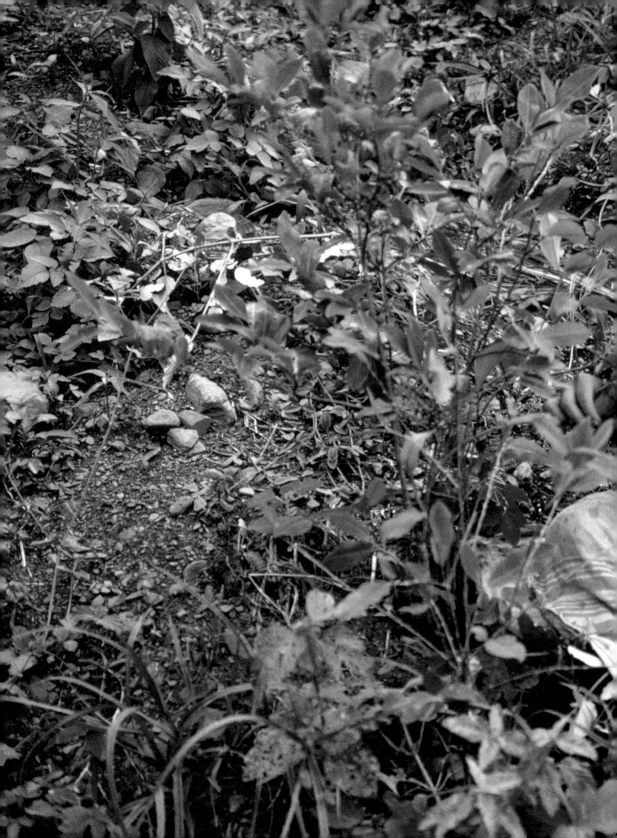

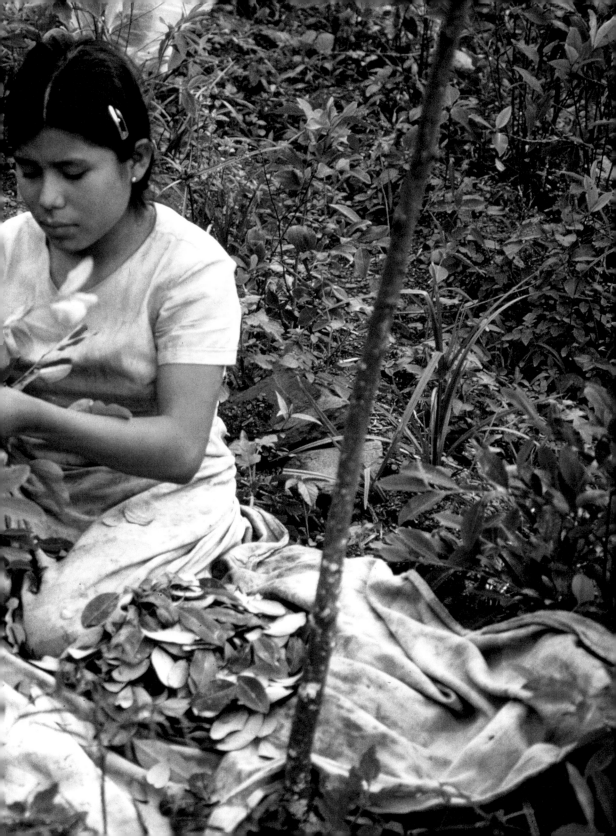

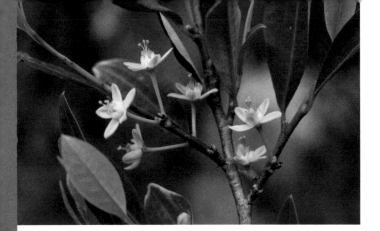

Fig. 37 (overleaf). Timothy Plowman and Wade Davis. Girl picking coca plant, *Erythoxylum coca*. Maranura, Province La Convención, Department of Cuzco, Peru, photographed before 1983. The Field Museum, B83352c.

Fig. 38 (above). Timothy Plowman. *Erythroxylum novogranatense* var. *truxillense*, or Trujillo coca plant. Collambay, Department La Libertad, Peru, photographed before 1983. The Field Museum, B83351c.

Fig. 39 (right). Martín Chambi. "Campesino Chewing Coca Leaves," photographed near Cuzco, Peru, 1939. Martín Chambi Family Archives.

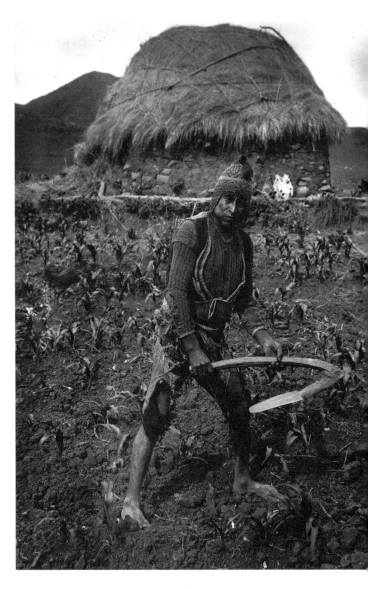

The Coca Leaf

Among the sacrifices of plants, vegetables and fruits of the land, none was as highly esteemed as coca.[60]

—Bernabe Cobo, *Inca Religion and Customs* (1609)

Although Father Bernabe Cobo wrote *Inca Religion and Customs* in the seventeenth century, his summary of coca's cultural importance in the Andes could equally apply 1,000 years earlier or 400 years later. Andean communities cultivate coca leaves for chewing, and the leaves and the act of chewing them have been central to daily life, ritual practice, politics, economics, and community solidarity for millennia.

For a plant so lauded through time, coca leaves are surprisingly nondescript. A low tree or shrub with small flowers and leaves that taper to a point, the coca plant belongs to the genus *Erythroxylum P. Browne*, which grows in many regions worldwide. Coca, however, is most extensively found in South America, where botanists have identified approximately two hundred species. There, coca leaf growers cultivate two species, each with two varieties: *Erythroxylum coca* var. *coca* (Huánuco coca) (fig. 37), *Erythroxylum coca* var. *ipadu* (Amazonian coca), *Erythroxylum novogranatense* var. *novogranatense* (Colombian coca), and *Erythroxylum novogranatense* var. *truxillense* (Trujillo coca) (fig. 38). Distinguished by particularities of bark, leaf, flower, and fruit, each variant is adapted to particular environments and favored by different markets.[61]

Cultivating and Consuming Coca in the Andes

Coca is a relatively hardy plant, and Andean farmers grow it on valley bottoms or artificial terraces built into hillsides.[62] Coca plants remain productive for as long as forty years and yield three to four harvests per year, with each bush producing roughly 500 grams of leaves per crop. In South America, with the exception of the Amazonian variety, people chew coca leaves whole. After harvesting, coca growers dry the leaves by laying them out in the sun, using a purpose-built oven, or toasting them in ceramic pans over a slow fire.[63] Once the leaves are dry, coca cultivators rehydrate them a little by sweating them in bales or cloth bags.

Coca leaves have a bitter, grassy flavor, so Andean people add an alkali substance (normally powdered lime, ashes, or baking soda) as a sweetener and stimulant. As the leaves and alkali mix with saliva, a "quid," or wad, of chewed leaves is formed, and this produces a visible bulge in the chewer's cheek. Note the coca quid in the right cheek of the farmer in figure 39. Depending on personal preference, habitual coca chewers keep the quid in their mouth for thirty to forty minutes and repeat the process roughly five times a day.[64]

Because of coca's importance, its cultivation has long been a major occupation for communities located near coca plantations.[65] Coca does not grow above a certain altitude, however, so communities in the high Andes must access it through long-distance networks of exchange, often mediated through complex systems of kinship and reciprocity. In these regions, people purchase

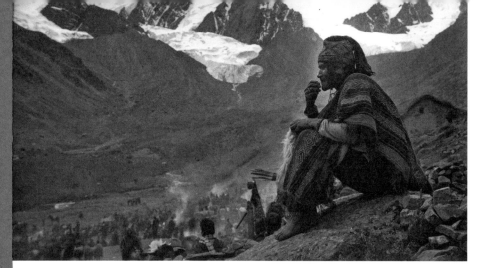

Fig. 40 (left).
Martín Chambi.
"Resting, Q'Olloriti."
Man chewing coca
after pilgrimage for
the Q'Olloriti Festival,
photographed 1935.
Martín Chambi Family
Archives.

Fig. 41 (opposite,
above). *Pacha Mama*
statue surrounded by
offerings of cigarettes,
candies, and coca leaves
in Calchaqui, Salta
Province, Argentina,
2005.

Fig. 42 (opposite,
below). Preparing
the *k'intus* during a
pago in Cerro Baúl,
Department of
Moquegua, Peru,
2010.

coca leaves, but sometimes they also exchange them for high-altitude products such as potatoes, fiber, and finished textiles.[66]

Physiological Effects of Chewing Coca

Although people outside the Andes are perhaps most familiar with coca as the source of cocaine, there are substantial differences between chewing coca leaves and ingesting concentrated extracted cocaine. There is no evidence that chewing coca leaves leads to a tolerance for cocaine or that it has any long-term deleterious effects on a person.[67] In fact, coca is a complex mix of alkaloids, flavonoids, and essential oils and minerals, which give coca leaves some nutritional value. Nonetheless, chewing coca leaves does result in a small amount of cocaine being absorbed through the buccal mucosa (the lining of the cheeks) and in the gastrointestinal tract, which is measurable in an individual's blood plasma approximately five minutes after chewing begins.[68] Even a tiny amount of absorbed cocaine produces temporary stimulation of the central nervous system, an effect that is increased by the addition of the alkali substance consumed with coca leaves.[69] Comparable in its short-term effects to drinking coffee and taking an aspirin, chewing coca leaves suppresses fatigue and hunger and increases energy levels.[70]

The chemical properties of coca are particularly beneficial to people living in high-altitude regions of the Andes, because many of its nutritious elements are otherwise lacking in regions where diets rely heavily on tubers and where fresh vegetables can be hard to come by. In an area of the world where temperatures can fall below freezing twenty-five nights of every month, the retention of body heat promoted by chewing coca is clearly desirable.[71] The thinner air at high altitudes makes strenuous activities especially taxing, and it is believed that coca's stimulating effects are useful in arduous work or in long-distance travel on foot (fig. 40).[72]

In addition to promoting regular chewing to offset the challenges of living in an extreme environment, local healers prescribe coca for a range of ailments. They suggest that placing chewed coca leaves on the eyelids relieves eye irritation; rubbing leaves mixed with animal fat onto the abdomen eases stomach ache; laying coca leaves on the temples alleviates a headache; gargling with a mixture of coca leaves and salt soothes a sore throat; and drinking an infusion of coca reduces the pain caused by tooth extraction. Coca is more widely known for its effectiveness in counteracting the nausea, headaches, and disorientation caused by altitude sickness, and guidebooks to the region often advise that visitors to the Andes drink coca tea to minimize its unpleasant symptoms.[73]

Coca as Social Substance

The social roles of coca in Andean communities are as important as its medicinal uses, and its cultural signifi-cance is reflected in songs, poems, and refrains.[74] Coca chewing even has its own origin myth, in which a *mamacha* (little mother) lost her child.[75] In the depths of grief, she pulled some leaves from a coca bush and began to chew them. Since then, the story goes, *Runa* (Quechua people) have chewed coca to alleviate pain and grief. Today, exchanging and chewing coca is a means to demonstrate and consolidate personal ties to others, to the land, and to the gods.

The Quechua word for the act of chewing coca is *hallpay*. In a practice akin to a coffee break, friends, family, and workmates take time out from their day to sit together and converse as they chew their leaves. Sharing coca is an integral component of *hallpay*, and even regular "coca breaks" involve a series of ceremonial actions and stylized refrains through which leaves are offered and accepted. Simultaneously routine and highly ritualized, sharing leaves and chewing together are expressions of friendship. Coca reaffirms existing social bonds and embeds individuals in ongo-ing relationships of reciprocity.

The process of sharing coca is repeated in numerous situations, such as when visitors pay a call on a family, when friends meet on the road, and before a relative begins a long journey. Exchanging and chewing coca also cement more noteworthy events. For example, individuals offered a political position, such as *alcalde* (mayor), will signal their acceptance of the position by accepting an offer of coca. Once in position, office holders aggrandize themselves during festivals by hosting feasts that involve large quantities of coca in addition to food and alcohol. Marriage proposals are sealed with coca shared by the two sets of prospective in-laws. Mourners share coca at funerals, and chewed coca may be thrown into a grave. Families also mark the remem-brance ceremonies that occur annually around All Saints Day by chewing and offering coca. During animal fertility rites, animals as well as people some-times consume coca when herds are force-fed leaves.[76]

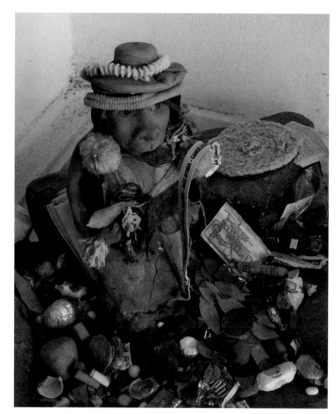

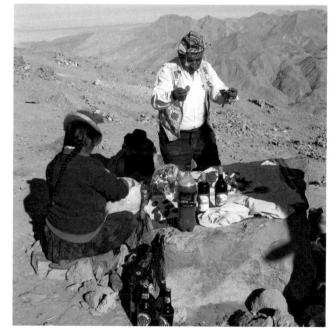

Coca in Spiritual Life

Across the Andes, offerings of coca leaves to mother earth (fig. 41) and to the mountain gods are an integral part of numerous dedicatory rituals, known in many regions by the Spanish word *pago* (payment). These ceremonies are a vital antecedent to house building, community construction projects, and even archaeological excavation and are conducted by local ritual specialists, variously called *curanderos* or *yatiri*. People also undertake *pagos* for more personal reasons, such as trying to win the heart of another, wishing to become pregnant, or trying to cure illness.[77]

During a *pago*, the *curandero* and his or her assistant spread coca leaves out on an *unkuña*,[78] a small square cloth, taking care that the leaves do not fall from the *unkuña* onto the ground (see cat. 2). They select the best specimens (green, unblemished leaves) in groups of at least three and place them on top of one another in an arrangement called a *k'intu* (fig. 42). The *curandero* hands a *k'intu* to each *pago* participant, who holds it between the right thumb and index finger. The participant raises the *k'intu* and blows on it, and then makes invocations to particular spirits, often the mountains of his or her home territory. The *curandero* gathers the *k'intus* and any remaining coca leaves, together with other offered items, including the fetus of a llama, flowers, various plants, animal fat, candies, and in some regions small, commercially prepared sets of offerings called *misas* (fig. 43). Once they have collected all of the offerings and blessed them in a series of rites incorporating both Andean and Catholic invocations, the *curandero* wraps them in a cloth bundle and burns them. *Pago* participants throw *chicha* (homemade maize beer), wine, and more coca leaves upon the fire. Soothsayers also use coca in divination rituals, reading the leaves to predict the future and determine auspicious dates for important events, including *pagos*.

Members of Andean communities may undertake elements of these rituals before carrying out more routine activities. Before friends share coca during a regular break from work, for example, they may prepare and blow upon *k'intus*.

Before weaving, a woman may blow on coca leaves and invoke the female saints.[79] During potato planting, farmers cut a cross in the top of the first seed potato and place coca leaves vertically in the cross before burying the potato.[80] A traveler passing by a sacred mountain will offer coca leaves to it, seeking to secure a safe journey, and miners who work in treacherous conditions in and around Potosi, Bolivia, assert that it is the Devil (*el Tío*) who protects them while they are underground, and they offer him coca at mine entrances (fig. 44).[81]

Chuspas: Enduring Symbols of Social Identity and Relationships

Given the centrality of coca leaves in interpersonal relationships and interactions, the act of wearing a bag that contains them can be understood as an important demonstration of community membership and engagement in the social practices described above. The aesthetic differences that distinguish *chuspas* from different regions, even from one village to another, indicate that an individual will assert an affiliation with a particular community by wearing a particular style of coca bag. However, wearing a *chuspa* is also indicative of individual identity and social standing within a community. Exactly who wears coca bags and what type of coca bag they wear varies regionally and even between neighboring villages.

Chewing coca is an activity that marks social maturity, and so its container is necessarily age restricted.[82] Although the formal presentation of a *chuspa* is no longer an integral part of coming-of-age ceremonies in the Andes today, it is still a textile that may be acquired only by individuals with a certain degree of maturity. Modern Peruvian weavers report that children (or boys, depending on gender limitations) begin wearing *chuspas* between the ages of eight and fifteen. A photograph of adult males and a younger boy taken by Grace Goodell during an ethnographic collection project for the AMNH in Oruro, Bolivia in 1968, suggests that boys there began to wear *chuspas* from a similar age to that described by weavers today (fig. 45).

Gender-based restrictions are more complex and variable. In several studies of

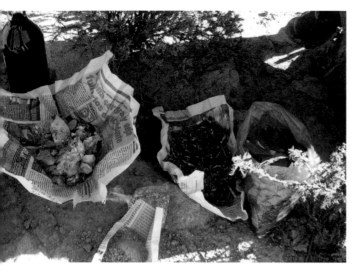

Fig. 43 (left). Pago offerings, including coca leaves (at right) in Camata, Department of Moquegua, Peru, 2006.

Fig. 44 (below). Miners chewing coca and offering it to the Devil (*el Tío*) in Potosi, Bolivia, 2001.

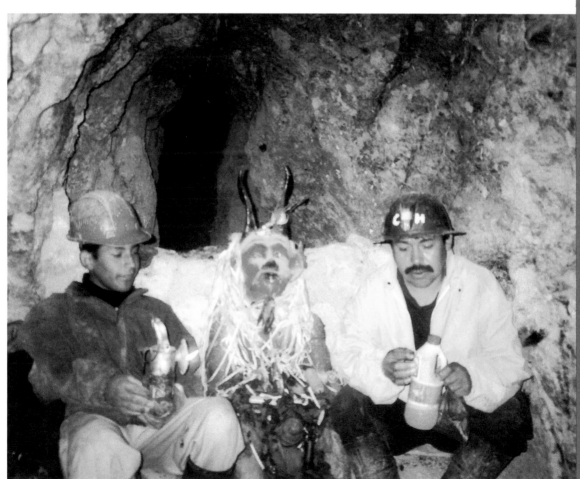

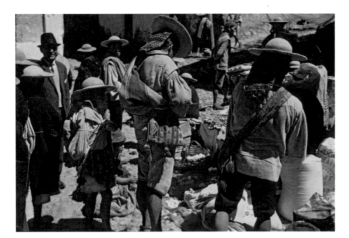

Fig. 45. Grace Goodell. Men and boys in a market, Bolivia, 1968. Courtesy of the Division of Anthropology Archives, American Museum of Natural History.

textiles and research about coca in the Andes today, scholars explicitly identify the coca bag as a male accoutrement.[83] However, this association is not universal and can vary even in villages located near one another.[84] In Quechua–speaking villages in the Department of Moquegua, *chuspas* are used only by men; women carry their coca in a carrying cloth, or *unkuña*. Yet in neighboring Aymara–speaking villages, gender proscriptions are absent and both men and women use coca bags.[85]

Where the wearing of a coca bag is not gender specific, construction details may differentiate men's and women's bags. For example, in addition to highly patterned woven bags, some contemporary communities, such as Q'ero, in the Department of Cuzco, also make coca bags called *phukucho* from the hide of a llama or an alpaca (fig. 46). From a distance or to the untrained eye, the *phukucho* carried by men and women are identical. However, men's bags are made from the front part of the skin of a baby camelid, and women's bags are constructed from the rear part.[86]

Ethno-historic and archaeological data indicate that gender flexibility in the use of coca bags is not a new practice. Some of the earliest known coca bags, those excavated from Nazca burials, were interred with females as well as males, a practice also evident a thousand years later in the Estuquiña tradition of southern Peru.[87]

Particular kinds of coca bags act as signifiers of status or occupation. Given the religious use of coca leaves, an associ-

ation between coca bags and ritual practitioners is to be expected. Mortuary data indicates that the earliest *chuspas* from northern Chile may have been restricted to shamans or other ritual specialists.[88] In Ausangate, in highland Peru, Andrea Heckman noted that camelid-hide coca bags, like the *phukucho* used in Q'ero, are worn only by religious practitioners.[89] Clearly, wearing a *chuspa* is not merely a practical means of carrying coca leaves but is also a means for asserting one's identity and position within society.

Not only emblems of personal identity and community affiliation, *chuspas* are integral to interactions with gods and with others. Whether shared with friends and relatives during a routine coca break or given to the gods during a *pago*, coca is correctly shared from a *chuspa*, and so its use is itself a display of etiquette.[90] To share a *chuspa* or to offer one as a gift, not just the leaves it holds, is an even more personal demonstration of a social relationship than simply chewing together,[91] although social norms governing the exchange of *chuspas* vary substantially from region to region. For example, in Q'ero, a girl might weave a coca bag for her sweetheart as a token of her affection.[92] On the Island of Taquile, where *chuspas* are carried only by married men, a new bride will weave a coca bag for her father-in-law, an intimacy considered akin to incest elsewhere.[9]

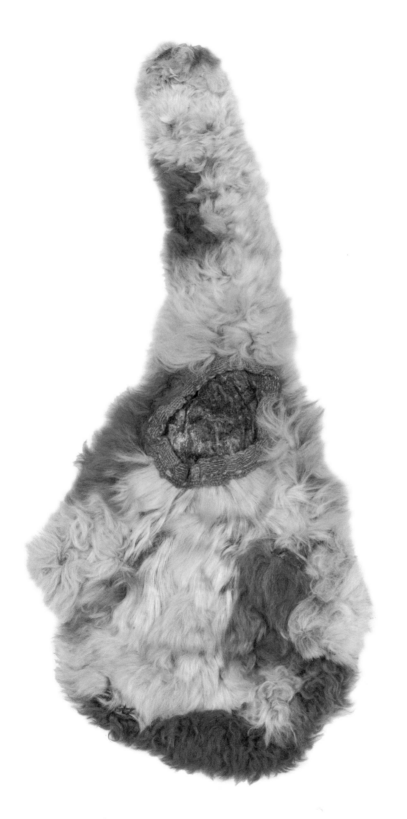

Fig. 46. *Phukucho* bag. Q'ero Village, Department of Cuzco, Peru, accessioned in 1956. Llama hide and fur. Courtesy of the Division of Anthropology, American Museum of Natural History, 40.0/8913. Cat. 22.

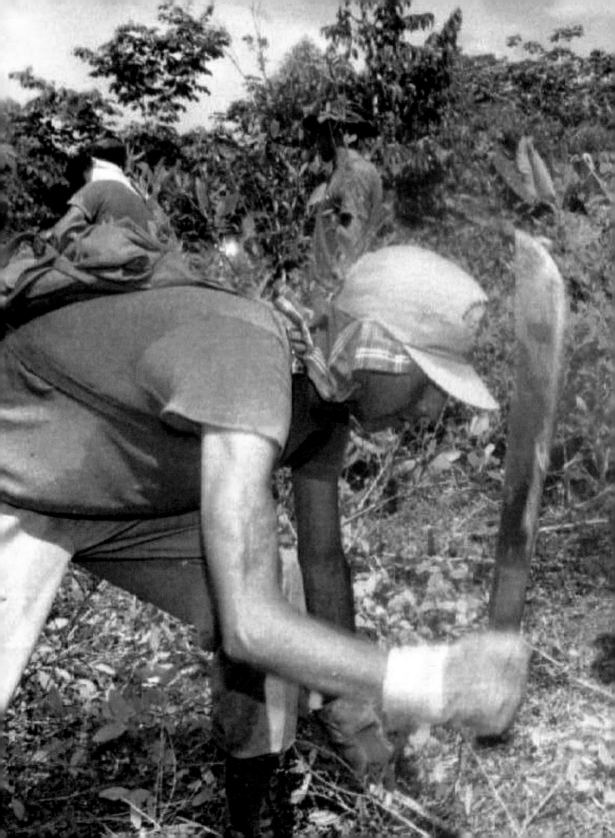

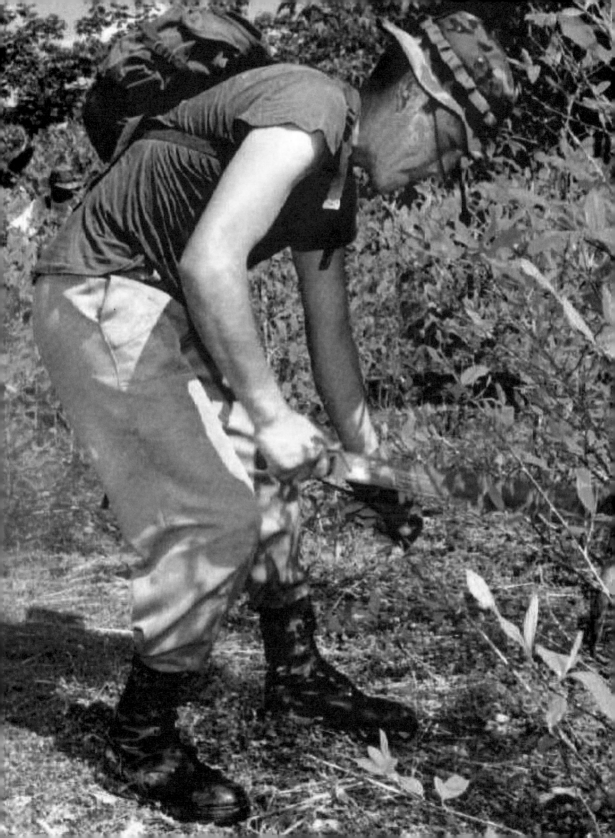

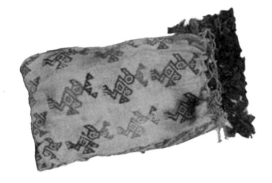

Fig. 47 (overleaf).
Antonio Bueno.
Destruction of coca
plants in Ivirgarzama,
Bolivia, 1998.
Associated Press.

Fig. 48 (above). Bag
with coca leaves.
Chancay culture,
central coast of Peru,
AD 1000–1400.
Cotton, camelid
fiber, fourcroya; plain
weave, supplementary
weft patterning (or
brocade), overcasting
stitches. Courtesy
of the Division
of Anthropology,
American Museum
of Natural History,
B/8661.

Fig. 49. *Llipta*
container depicting a
prisoner. Wari, Peru,
AD 600–1000. Wood,
bone inlay, paint. The
Metropolitan Museum
of Art, Purchase,
Rogers Fund and Carol
R. Meyer and Arthur
M. Bullowa Gifts, 1977
(1977.376).

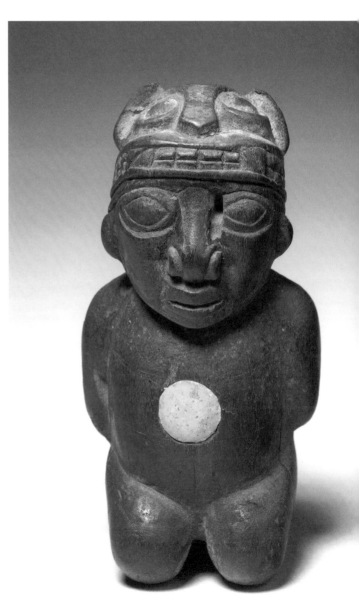

Coca through Time: Deep Roots and Changing Perceptions

Like textiles, coca has a long history in the Andes. Coca leaves have occupied a central place in the adaptive strategies, economic systems, social networks, and ritual practices of Andean communities for millennia. Archaeological data identify the antiquity of coca cultivation, and colonial documents and ethnographic accounts reveal the deep roots of coca's multiple roles in Andean communities. However, since the Spanish conquest, coca has become a contested and legislated substance, at times sought after by the West, at other times demonized. It is not only embedded in cultural traditions, but it is also increasingly embroiled in global politics. In the following section I explore the many ways in which *chuspas* have been used and perceived over the years within the long and complex history of coca.

The Archaeological Record

People probably discovered the stimulating properties of Huánuco coca, the ancestral form of cultivated coca, shortly after they first inhabited the eastern Andes some seven thousand years ago and began to transplant coca plants to areas near their homes. As human populations moved across the landscape, they carried coca, and this resulted in isolation and gradual differentiation between species and varieties as the plant adapted to new environments.[94]

Physical evidence for coca in the archaeological record comes in the form of leaves and endocarps, the hard layer surrounding the seed or pit of a plant.[95] Archaeologists have tentatively identified coca leaves from several sites along the coast of Peru dating to the end of the Late Pre-Ceramic Period (3000–1800 BC).[96] Excavators recovered the earliest definite leaves and endocarps from Vista Alegre, a site dating to AD 600–1000 in the Rimac Valley near modern Lima. Further south, researchers working in northern Chile have found entire bags of coca leaves dating to the Cabuzas culture (AD 400–1000), and museum collections around the world contain examples of later bags and bundles containing coca (fig. 48).

In the 1980s, archaeologists excavating sites dating to the Late Intermediate Period (AD 1000–1460) in the Upper Mantaro Valley in Peru recovered endocarps from Huánuco coca in the trash pits of elite domestic structures. This discovery is particularly interesting to scholars because the structures are located 3,000 meters above sea level, far above the cultivation range of coca, indicating that, as it is now, coca was an important exchange item in pre-Hispanic times.[97]

Techniques derived from the medical sciences confirm that pre-Hispanic populations actually consumed coca. A technique called radioimmunoassay can identify cocaine's metabolite (benzoylecgonine) in human hair. When scientists applied this technique to mummies from northern Chile, they found that although the earliest tested mummies from the Chinchorro culture (7000–2000 BC) had no cocaine metabolite in their bodies, it was present in individuals from

350 BC on.[98] Coca consumption increased through time and analyses of mummies from about AD 1000 identified benzoylecgonine in infants as well as in adult males and females, suggesting that the metabolite passed from mother to child through the placenta. Coca consumption across populations continued into the Inca Period (1400–1533).[99]

Indirect archaeological correlates for coca consumption exist in the apparatus associated with coca chewing, such as *llipta* jars, small vessels that contained the lime or other alkaloid substances chewed with coca. Many of the surviving examples are made of non-perishable materials, especially stone or ceramic, although wooden examples also survive (fig. 49). The earliest identified likely *llipta* container is a bottle gourd from the Valdivia culture in Ecuador dated to 2100 BC.[100]

Pictures of individuals chewing coca are also common in many pre-Hispanic craft traditions. The earliest of these depictions dates to 1600 BC in Ecuador: a modeled human figurine with a coca quid in its cheek.[101] Ceramic figurines with similar coca quids are also known for, among others, the Moche (AD 1–550), the Tiwanaku (AD 600–1000) (fig. 50), the Chimu (see cat. 1), and the Inca, who also produced them in gold and silver (fig. 51).[102]

The context in which archaeologists find coca reveals the antiquity of its social, ritual, and economic roles. Excavators frequently recover coca from pre-Hispanic tombs, and some Maitas Chribaya burials (AD 1000–1250) in northern Chile contain mummies with quids of coca in their mouths.[103] Scholars excavating a Tiwanaku (AD 600–1000) structure in the Moquegua Valley, in southern Peru, found a mummified guinea pig buried with coca leaves, evidence that ritually offering coca leaves is a centuries-old practice.[104] *Chuspas* themselves are an important piece of the archaeological story of coca, and significantly the context of their discovery affirms the longevity of *chuspas'* roles in ritual and funerary practice. Archaeologists have uncovered small, plain-weave bags of coca strung together in sets buried under a temple at Pachacamac, a pre-Hispanic multi-period oracle

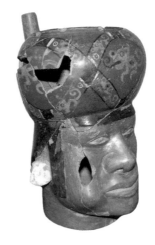

Fig. 50. Tiwanaku portrait vessel depicting a man with coca quid in his cheek. Excavated on the Island of Pariti, Lake Titicaca, Bolivia, AD 600–1000. Ceramic. Antti Korpisaari, PRT 00071.

site located south of Lima. Although the exact meaning of the bags remains elusive, their location suggests that they were small, expendable talismans.[105]

Most extant pre-Hispanic *chuspas*, including many of the bags illustrated in this essay, were recovered from burials. It is important, however, to note that the inclusion of a coca bag in a tomb is not unequivocal evidence that the interred individual chewed coca. A comparison of biological and textile data from tombs in northern Chile revealed that even individuals who had not consumed coca were buried with *chuspas*.[106] In this context, then, the *chuspa* was a marker of community identity, not evidence of the personal habits of the deceased, and its inclusion in a burial merely indicates the importance of coca in cultural practice.

The Inca Empire

The topic of coca appears repeatedly in documents written during the sixteenth and seventeenth centuries, after the Spanish conquest of the Andes. Colonial Period documents that draw on statements made by native individuals who had lived under Inca rule shed light on the production and consumption of coca during the final decades of the pre-Hispanic period. As the Inca Empire expanded to the coast from its highland center in Cuzco, ruling Inca elites appropriated pre-existing coastal coca plantations in order to access the coca necessary for state rituals. Coca cultivation was so important to imperial authorities that the

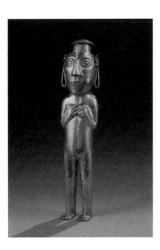

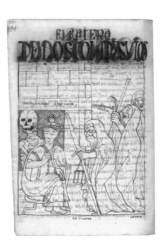

Fig. 51 (far left). Figurine of elite male with coca quid in left cheek. Inca, Peru, 1450–1540. Silver. Dumbarton Oaks, Pre-Columbian Collection, Washington, DC, PC.B.474.

Fig. 52 (left). Felipe Guaman Poma de Ayala. "Burials of the Condesuyos," page 297, drawing 116. From *El primer nueva corónica y buen gobierno*, 1615–16. Condesuyo refers to one of the four territories of the Inca Empire. Det Kongelige Bibliotek, Copenhagen, Denmark.

state transplanted agriculturalists from their homes to new locations specifically in order to farm coca fields.[107]

Then, as today, people used coca extensively in a range of imperial, community, and household rituals and coca was a plant that merited its own dedicated ceremonies. People even fasted from it at particular times of the year.[108] Like earlier cultures, the Incas offered coca leaves to the gods, and they used them in initiation ceremonies.[109] According to Bernabe Cobo, coca was "offered in many ways. Sometimes the whole coca [leaf] was offered, and at other times the leaf was offered after it had been chewed and the juice sucked out. Sacrifices were made to the Earth by scattering coca on it."[110]

As in earlier periods, coca was central to Inca funerary practices, and *chuspas* were important carriers of coca to tombs (fig. 52). They were included in grave offerings, even in one of the most extreme celebrations of death in the Inca Empire, a ritual called *capacocha*, which was undertaken for particularly important events, such as the inauguration of a new emperor. The most elaborate *capacocha* events included sacrificing children on mountain peaks. Commonly sacrificed in pairs of a male and a female, the children were physically flawless and often the offspring of local lords. Inca officials marched these children, who were dressed in fine clothes, hundreds of miles across the empire to the summit of a snow-capped mountain. There the officials drugged and killed the children before burying them where they died.

Because of the sub-zero conditions in which many of these sacrifices took place, several examples of *capacocha* child sacrifice are preserved almost intact; the best known are from southern Peru, northern Chile, and northern Argentina.[111] Fine pottery, coca leaves, and sumptuary goods were buried with the children.[112] Coca bags recovered from *capacocha* are particularly elaborate and often made of feathers, the most esteemed cloth in the empire (fig. 53).[113] *Capacocha* funerary assemblages also include tiny human figurines carved from spondylus shell and crafted in gold and silver, each dressed in Inca attire and equipped with miniature *chuspas*.[114]

Wearing a *chuspa* as an important symbol of identity in the Inca Empire, as it is today, but it was a more explicit symbol of maturity than it is now. Describing a male initiation ritual at the town of Copacabana on the shores of Lake Titicaca, the seventeenth-century chronicler Ramos Gavilan recounted how each community brought its boys thirteen or fourteen years of age to a public place, where they competed in races. The boys who won were rewarded with a *chuspa*, a symbol of manhood and of membership in the Inca state.[115]

Chuspas appear to have been components of both male and female dress in the Inca Empire. Early Quechua dictionaries distinguish between the word for a man's coca bag and that for a woman's,[116] but Guaman Poma's drawings of Inca nobles depict both men and women wearing very similar bags (fig. 54). The

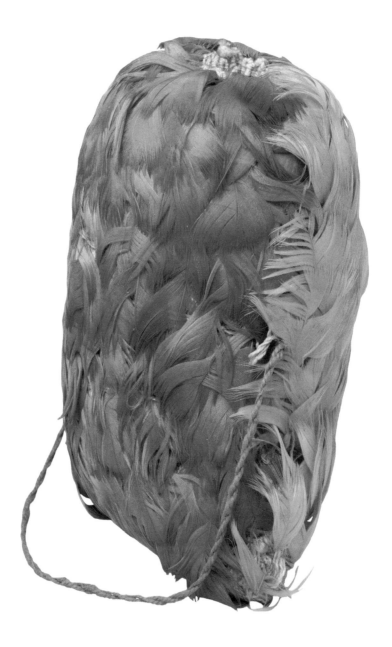

Fig. 53. Feathered
bag. Inca, Peru, 15th–
early 16th century.
Feathers, cotton. The
Metropolitan Museum of
Art, Purchase, Bequest of
Arthur M. Bullowa, 1993
(1994.35.101).

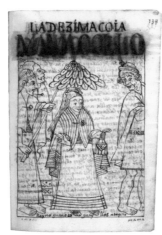

Fig. 54. Felipe Guaman Poma de Ayala. "Mama Ocllo, the 10th Inca Queen," page 138, drawing 48. From *El primer nueva corónica y buen gobierno*, 1615–16. Det Kongelige Bibliotek, Copenhagen, Denmark.

fact that nobles are wearing *chuspas* in Guaman Poma's drawings contributes to confusion over the degree to which coca and *chuspas* were socially restricted in the Inca Empire. Early Colonial documentary data suggests that *chuspas* were an important sign of political office in the Inca Empire.[117] Further, the Jesuit brother Jose de Acosta observed in 1590 that coca was a privilege of Inca royals; this has been repeated at length in secondary literature and has led some authors to suggest that during the Inca Period *chuspas* were in fact restricted to elites.[118]

However, more detailed analyses of sixteenth-century documents contradict Acosta's assertion that only imperial leaders were allowed to chew coca. Instead, they indicate that although coca was a sumptuary item, even ordinary households had some access to it.[119] Given the persuasive documentary and archaeological challenges to the idea that coca was a privilege reserved solely for nobles, the claim that *chuspas* were also strictly restricted is problematic. More convincing is the suggestion that certain types of coca bags denoted status. In particular, a variant called a "pendant bag" likely acted as insignia of Inca royalty. Very finely woven and constructed from at least four separate sections, pendant bags have long red fringes and camelid iconography (fig. 55). The red fringe is reminiscent of a *mayscaypacha*, which Inca emperors wore on their foreheads. *Mayscaypachas* were strict symbols of imperial authority, and the idea that fringed bags were also royal markers is persuasive.[120]

Colonial Debates

Sixteenth- and seventeenth-century sources also reveal the debates that raged between Spanish colonists over coca based on conflicts rooted in the competing demands of religious fervor and economic common sense.[121] Reports were often, although not always, written with an explicit bias against the indigenous population.[122] Many of these documents emphatically condemned the use of coca on the grounds that it was integral to the very belief system that the Spaniards, particularly those with a proselytizing mission, sought to stamp out. Indeed, some early writers directly equated coca chewing with devil worship.[123] One goes as far as to state: "All those who chew coca are sorcerers who speak to demons; whether drunk or not they go crazy by chewing coca. May God save us. Sacraments cannot be given to those who chew coca."[124]

An evocative drawing of a sorcerer and a frightening figure with devilish characteristics accompanies this decisive statement (fig. 56). For those who saw coca as an impediment to the important mission of converting the native Andean population to Catholicism, the answer was simple—ban the production and consumption of the leaf—and so in 1552 the first ecclesiastical council in Lima condemned coca.[125]

Others, however, argued that coca was necessary for Spanish commercial interests. Recognizing the stimulating effects of coca, its colonial defenders put an economic spin on their argument,

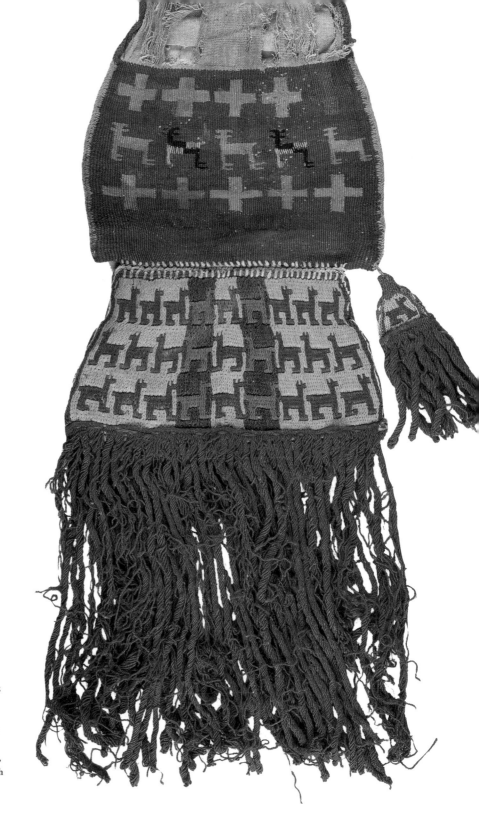

Fig. 55. Pendant coca
bag. South coast,
Peru, 1400–1600.
Camelid fiber, cotton;
looping, netting,
interlocked tapestry,
complementary warp
weave, plied fringe.
Museum of Fine Arts,
Boston, The Elizabeth
Day McCormick
Collection, 51.2452.

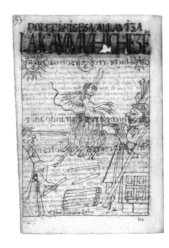

Fig. 56. Felipe Guaman Poma de Ayala. "High priests, walla wisa, layqha, umu, sorcerer," page 279, drawing 108. From *El primer nueva corónica y buen gobierno*, 1615–16. Det Kongelige Bibliotek, Copenhagen, Denmark.

asserting that the coca leaf would ensure the productivity of the hundreds of thousands of Andean laborers who worked for colonial landowners, particularly in the silver mines that were a primary source of wealth in the New World.[126] In fact, the Spaniards who had been granted agricultural land that included coca plantations found themselves in control of an extremely valuable crop.[127] Coca production increased as much as fiftyfold in the early Colonial Period, and despite ecclesiastical condemnation, the Church received substantial tithes from the profits of coca plantations.[128] Ultimately, the economic arguments won out. In 1573 Viceroy Toledo removed controls on coca production, and by the middle of the seventeenth century, debates within the viceroyalty largely ceased and coca opponents were effectively silenced.

Coca chewing was not, however, adopted as a means for increasing the work output of Europeans in South America. In the early Colonial Period, Spaniards controlled the coca trade and specifically marketed coca to native workers.[129] Although legislative discussion about coca underwent a three-hundred–year hiatus in Peru, the perception that coca chewing was suitable only for the lower, native classes held strong throughout the intervening centuries, as revealed in John James von Tschudi's 1854 comment that he knew "several persons of high respectability in Lima" who chewed coca but that "they could not do this openly, because among the refined class of Peruvians the *chacchar*

[chewing coca] is looked upon as a low and vulgar practice, befitting only to the laboring Indians."[130]

As noted above, *chuspas* from the seventeenth century are remarkably similar to their pre-Hispanic predecessors. Arguably, much of the conservatism seen in *chuspas* in the Colonial Period and later, relative to other textile forms, can be understood through the social connotations that developed around coca in that period. With coca chewing denigrated as a lower class and specifically "Indian" activity, the maintenance of non-European techniques, materials, and motifs in *chuspas* is perhaps unsurprising. Indeed, there is some historical evidence that *chuspas* were marked as class- and ethnic-specific soon after the Spanish conquest. In an analysis of women's wills from the sixteenth and seventeenth centuries, the historian Ana María Presta suggests that Andean women seeking to redefine their social standing in a changing world would carry discarded *chuspas*, so visibly and sensually Andean, in favor of "the patterned velvet bag decorated with silk and silver," materials with overt European overtones.[131] Since small European–style purses could easily have accommodated coca leaves, it is likely that they became popular among socially ambitious individuals as a means of hiding that denigrated activity.

European Interest Reawakened
The nineteenth century witnessed a rise in travel to Andean South America by Europeans, some of whom tried coca

and reported on it favorably.[132] As early as 1859, Pablo Mantegazza, an Italian physician who had practiced medicine in Peru, described his own experience with coca: "Borne on the wings of two coca leaves, I flew about in the spaces of 77,438 worlds, one more splendid than another"[133] and began entreating his European colleagues to use coca for medicinal purposes.[134] Coinciding with the development of alkaloid science in Europe, these descriptions and entreaties inspired efforts by researchers in the West to identify the plant's active principle, a feat achieved in 1860 by Albert Niemann when he isolated cocaine. In the following decades, scientists, including a young Sigmund Freud, explored the medicinal uses of coca, and Karl Koller's 1884 discovery of cocaine's anesthetic properties would later prove to be a revolutionary breakthrough.[135]

At the same time, entrepreneurs were incorporating coca into commercial medicinal wines. The most successful of these in the late nineteenth century was a Corsican named Angelo Mariani, who produced Vin Mariani, a combination of coca leaves and Bordeaux wine.[136] In his 1892 promotional pamphlet "Coca and its Therapeutic Application," Mariani described the beneficial effects of coca on a range of ailments and listed his various coca products. In addition to the classic Vin Mariani, which included carefully selected coca leaves from three sources, Mariani offered consumers Elixir Mariani, a beverage that not only had a higher alcohol content than his standard preparation but was also "three times as highly charged" with coca leaves; Pate Mariani (lozenges of coca); Pastilles Mariani (coca and cocaine, which differed from the lozenges "only by the addition of two milligrammes of Cocaine hydrochlorate to each pastille"[137]); and Thé Mariani, which could also be used as a gargle or throat spray. Mariani's concoctions were promoted heavily in advertisements and received celebrity endorsements from, among others, Thomas Edison, Sarah Bernhardt, and Pope Leo III (fig. 57).[138]

In the United States, John Pemberton, a pharmacist from Atlanta, launched his own version of coca wine in 1886, which he called Peruvian Wine Cola.

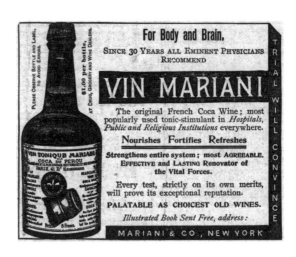

Shortly afterward, the manufacturers of this increasingly popular beverage removed wine from the product and added African kola nut. They named the new drink Coca-Cola. As its popularity took off, the United States began importing 600 to 1,000 metric tons of coca each year, most of it used to make the popular new drink. Cocaine was removed from Coca-Cola in 1903, but coca leaves are still important to the beverage's production. Today, Merchandise No. 5, a secret formula that includes extract of coca leaf, constitutes an essential flavoring in the soft drink.[139]

Prohibition Movement and Anti-Coca Legislation
Peru rose to meet the global demand for coca and cocaine in the late nineteenth century and became the world's biggest supplier of both.[140] However, despite Western commercial interest in the coca leaf, and despite vocal promotion by its supporters, international attitudes toward coca changed rapidly.[141] A growing awareness of the dangers of cocaine resulted in many American states passing anti-cocaine laws in the first decade of the twentieth century. Over the next half century, cocaine and coca imports came under increasingly strict federal legislation, and the United States began to exert pressure on other Western nations that had been involved in the export and commercialization of coca and cocaine.[142]

In Peru the influence of foreign anti-narcotic legislation resulted in a domestic prohibition movement that

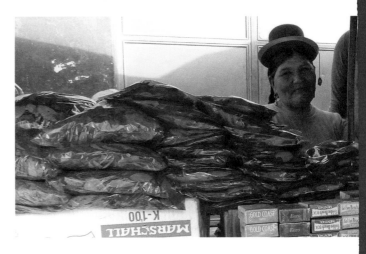

Fig. 57 (opposite).
Advertisement for "Vin
Mariani—The original
French coca wine,"
Harper's Weekly, 1893.
Bettmann/CORBIS.

Fig. 58. Coca for sale
(in green plastic bags)
in the city market,
Department of
Moquegua, Peru, 2013.

demonized the coca leaf.[143] The leader of this movement, Carlos Gutierrez-Noriega, blamed coca for numerous ills in native Andean communities, among them poor health, illiteracy, poverty, and "moral decay."[144] Although defenders of the coca leaf responded to what they saw as misplaced and damaging condemnation by documenting its important social roles in the Andes, the global community largely concurred with Gutierrez-Noriega's stance.[145] Between 1947 and 1950, the United Nations sponsored an investigation entitled "Mission of Enquiry into the Problem of the Coca Leaf." The commission's findings recommended that coca cultivation be phased out. In 1961 Peru and Bolivia, along with numerous other nations, signed the U.N.'s Single Convention on Narcotic Drugs. Among other things, the convention designated the coca leaf a narcotic drug and included articles requiring that signatories uproot wild coca plants, destroy coca bushes that were illegally cultivated, and, most contentiously, abolish coca-leaf chewing within twenty-five years.[146]

The devastating and terrifying cocaine epidemic that hit the United States and Europe in the 1980s and the violence and vast sums of money associated with the illicit cocaine trade[147] further animated critics of the coca leaf, who argued that it validated coca-eradication programs in Andean nations (see fig. 47).[148]

The extensive and intensive destruction of coca-leaf fields during the past several decades has had very real effects on the communities that have produced and used coca for centuries.[149] In the words of Catherine Allen, who has conducted the most thorough ethnographic study of coca in the Andes, members of these communities "must work in their fields all day without chewing coca leaves or exchanging *k'intus* in *hallpay*. . . .[T]heir burnt offerings are now meager, composed of carefully hoarded leaves" often bought on the black market for inflated prices, which "makes them angry."[150]

The anger and resentment at what has been perceived as a willful inability on the part of the West to separate cocaine from the coca leaf and as a total disregard for millennia-old cultural traditions have fueled largely left-leaning and indigenous political movements in Andean South America.[151] The most successful of these resulted in Evo Morales's winning the Bolivian presidency in 2005. The first Bolivian leader of indigenous heritage, Morales learned politics as the leader of a coca-leaf growers' union and has in the past declared that his political party, MAS (Movement toward Socialism), "grew out of the fight for coca."[152] Although the 1961 U.N. Convention is now more than fifty years old, it continues to be a source of contention for the Bolivian government. In 2011 Bolivia withdrew from the Convention and only re-acceded in February 2013 with the reservation that it does not accept the requirement for banning coca leaf chewing.[153]

Despite ongoing attempts to limit the production and circulation of coca,

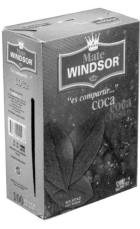

Fig. 59. "Mate Windsor" coca tea box, with the slogan "es compartir." Peru, 2011. Cardboard. Private collection. Cat. 33.

both the leaves and their derivative products continue to be highly visible commodities in Andean markets today (fig. 58). Commercially produced coca teas are widely available in South American towns and cities. They are made by brand-name companies and sold in chain stores alongside other teas and coffees. Recognizing the strongly held cultural associations of coca, the companies that market these products emphasize not only the restorative effects of coca but also its social functions. Notice the phrasing that continues to reference the deep-seated etiquette of coca chewing in the label on the box in figure 59, which asserts that coca tea is "something to be shared."

Altered Materials: Plastic Bags

The repackaging of coca includes the leaves as well as derivative products. For generations, some communities have differentiated between fiesta *chupsas* and *chuspas* for daily use; compare the bags in figure 34 and checklist number 5. Both bags are from the village of Q'ero and date to the mid-twentieth century, but the bag in the checklist is an elaborated version, with additional pockets indicating that it was made for use in fiestas.[154] However, in many Andean communities today, people use woven coca bags only during fiestas, which is particularly noticeable where *chuspas* are created specifically for men. In some regions, men wear "western" or "street" clothes, except for special occasions, whereas women wear "ethnic" dress on a daily basis.[155]

For example, in the Department of Moquegua, it is common to see women wearing elaborate highland outfits, even in the heavily mestizo departmental capital city, but it is unusual to see a man dressed in local costume unless he is a dancer prepared for a performance. Weavers in this region comment that they occasionally see an older person with a *chuspa,* but that the simple plastic bags in which coca leaves are sold have largely replaced the elaborate woven bags. *Chuspas* are still used on special occasions in which local dress is worn by men and women, at least by men who are performing.[156] In fact, because *chuspas* are produced less frequently, even within regions such as Moquegua, where weaving continues to be an important and visible craft activity, the channels by which a person obtains a *chuspa* are altered. If necessary, a man can rent a *chuspa* at the rate of five soles a day (approximately two U.S. dollars), instead of relying on one made by a female relative or a close acquaintance.[157]

Our understanding of the antiquity of coca-related practices in the Andes is based in large part on the fact that woven *chuspas* survived for centuries in pre-Hispanic burials. The practice of interring a *chuspa* with the dead continues into the present in some communities. In the recent past, in Aymara–speaking communities in the Department of Moquagua, when an individual who had particularly enjoyed chewing coca died, his or her relatives would bury the person with a hand-crafted coca bag. However, with the decreasing use of *chuspas* on a daily basis, and the greater reliance on disposable plastic bags today, mourners often place a plastic bag full of leaves in a grave instead of beautifully woven textile bags, which require a great investment of time and material.[158]

Altered Contexts:
"*Chuspas*" beyond the Andes

Although woven *chuspas,* which fulfilled a range of important cultural roles within Andean societies for hundreds of years, have in recent times been replaced to a large degree by plastic in Peru and Bolivia, they have found a new life beyond the Andes. One example of this is a bag called a *chuspa* produced in 2013 for sale in the tourist market in Arequipa (fig. 60). Its construction and consumption mark it as vastly different from the bags described in this essay, and although this textile was sold as a *chuspa*, the bag itself is a world away from its namesake.

Compare manufacture with the spinning, weaving, and embellishing process described for hand-crafted bags. The bag in figure 60 was constructed in parts. Its body is made of fabric imported from another Peruvian city, Puno, and even though the colors appear similar to the natural fibers of camelids, the cloth is synthetic and machine woven. It is patterned with images recognizable to even the most poorly informed visitor as "Andean," but the designs have little specific relevance to Arequipa. The roughly executed image of the Staff God is a figure that most famously decorates a stone gate at the Bolivian site of Tiwanaku. To give the textile a local quality, after the cloth arrived in Arequipa, local manufactures cut it into pieces and embellished it with machine embroidery, including the name of the city over an image of a mountain reminiscent of Misti, the snow-capped peak for which Arequipa is famous. Beneath the mountain, they embroidered "Peru" in the colors of the national flag. Because the bag was created specifically for tourists, its makers added a padding and black synthetic cloth liner, along with a zipped pocket placed between the padding and lining. They then sewed the back and front pieces together and added a synthetic, store-bought strip as both edging and strap. The longer back piece

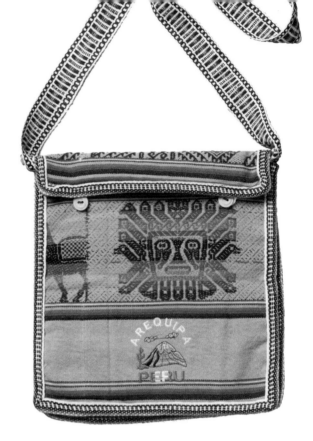

Fig. 60. Tourist "*chuspa*." Arequipa, Peru, 2013. Synthetic fibers, zipper, wooden buttons; machine-made, with embroidery. Private collection. Cat. 32.

folds over to create a flap, which is closed with two small wooden buttons. There is nothing "*chuspa*" about this contemporary Peruvian bag, but the style has become widely distributed worldwide.

The growing commercial market for *chuspas* within the souvenir trade has resulted in a change in the ways they are circulated as well as in production practices. With the explosion of Internet access, the commodity market for *chuspas* no longer remains geographically limited. Instead of being an object carefully crafted for a close relative, today's *chuspas* are mass produced and sold not only in Andean tourist destinations but also across the globe. A quick search online for "*chuspa,*" "coca bag," or "Peruvian bag" produces numerous opportunities for a global consumer to choose from a variety of coca bag styles, such as the examples in figure 61. These bags are simultaneously sold as *chuspas* in Arequipa and other Andean destinations and online as "tote bags." Divorced from their intended use for carrying coca leaves, and also from the local and regional significance of the motifs that decorate them, these bags have been reinvented and re-made for tourists to serve as book bags, shopping bags, or purses.

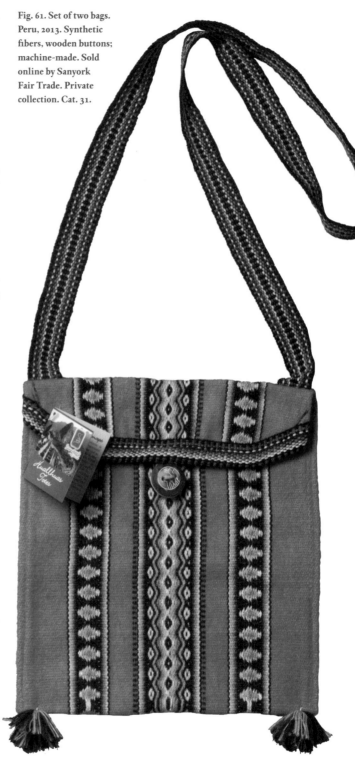

Fig. 61. Set of two bags. Peru, 2013. Synthetic fibers, wooden buttons; machine-made. Sold online by Sanyork Fair Trade. Private collection. Cat. 31.

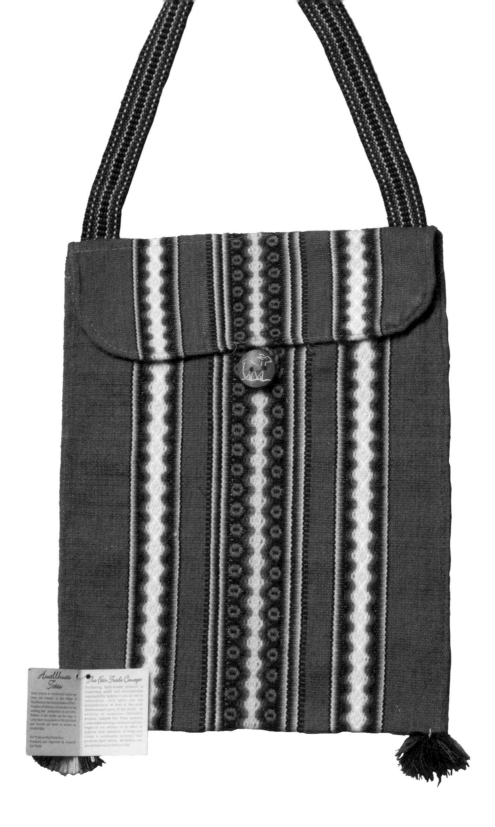

Conclusion

All craft objects are both products of their makers and material interjections in social life. For thousands of years, elaborately woven textiles have been one of the most highly regarded and important media for artistic expression in Andean South America. However, the adaptive and social roles of textiles in this context are just as important as their aesthetic value. Their significance is further accentuated when they intersect with other essential cultural products. This is perhaps most apparent in *chuspas*. By physically and metaphorically uniting coca leaves with woven cloth, *chuspas* are uniquely Andean.

An enduring and widespread object, the *chuspa* expresses an aesthetic that serves as a testament to the particular time and place in which it was made, and its material presence offers a visual chronology of Andean weaving traditions. Across time and space *chuspas* have long served social functions beyond their use as carriers of coca by communicating social and cultural affiliations, denoting their wearer's gender, and signifying his or her occupational, regional, linguistic, and ethnic identity. *Chuspas* act as conduits for relationships between people and between people and their gods. They are stages on which religious and political ideology is displayed. Through their function and the context of their various uses, *chuspas* have given Andean people a way to construct, reconstruct, and contest their social worlds for millennia.

Today *chuspas* face their most radical reinvention. In exploring the ways in which indigenous and mestizo populations in the Andes use cultural practices to differentiate from one other, Catherine Allen noted in 1988 that "Coca signifies Indian-ness: 'Only Runakuna chew coca.'"[159] Yet it is not necessarily Runakuna (Quechua people) who carry *chuspas* now, as *chuspas* have been largely replaced by disposable and forgettable plastic containers, and woven bags are increasingly directed toward a growing external market. In an international context in which coca leaves are derided but handicrafts are lauded and desired, the unique meaning of *chuspas* is increasingly diminished as they are divorced from the very substance that has defined and distinguished them for centuries.

Afterword: Exhibiting *Chuspas*

The coca bags and other objects that illustrate this essay are currently housed in museums around the world. The examples exhibited in *Carrying Coca* are part of the permanent South American collections at the American Museum of Natural History in New York City. The AMNH's long history of research in Andean South America began in 1892, and the museum has extensive collections of archaeological and ethnographic material from the region.[160] Included among the Andean textiles at the AMNH are about one hundred coca bags, representing fifteen centuries of weaving traditions. Resituating the exhibited bags in time and space was a vital stage in the development of this exhibition, a process in part dependent on the museum records for each piece.

The exhibited coca bags include objects that museum staff accessioned as long ago as 1894 and as recently as 1988. Although the museum acquired many of these objects as gifts or purchases, several were accessioned as a result of four research expeditions in the Andes, which merit brief discussion here. Spanning the years 1892 to 1968, the expeditions reflect the AMNH's long-standing interest in Andean textile arts, and they also reveal shifting motivations and changes in collections practice. A comparison of the four expeditions and the associated archives highlights the considerable variation in the documentation surrounding individual objects and exemplifies the ways in which research methodologies in the field have long-term implications for scholarship on museum collections.

Henry Villard Expedition to Peru, 1892–94
The Bandelier collection remains one of the most famous and extensive collections of Andean archaeological material now housed at the AMNH. The explorer and archaeologist Adolph Bandelier acquired the collection in the late nineteenth century in South America. Beginning in 1892, Bandelier spent a total of eleven years in Peru and Bolivia and conducted research at some of the most important pre-Hispanic sites in the region. He augmented his work with maps and photographs that documented not only sites but also landscapes and people (see fig. 19). During the first two years, Bandelier's fieldwork was funded by Henry Villard, a German immigrant who made his money in the railroad business. When Villard became temporarily bankrupt, the AMNH took over Bandelier's expedition, and the materials collected between 1892 and 1894 were donated to the museum to ensure that they would be cared for along with the materials Bandelier subsequently collected under the direct sponsorship of the museum.[161] Although Bandelier exported to the United States large quantities of archaeological material from numerous sites during his years in the Andes, the provenance of many of the pieces is limited. It is even difficult to determine where and how Bandelier acquired the three objects exhibited here (see cats. 4, 6, 11). The correspondence and customs paperwork associated with the Bandelier collection suggest that all three objects were included in a large shipment that Bandelier sent to New York from

Lima in August 1892. The miniature bag that is checklist number 6 is listed as coming from Ancon, a large multi-period archaeological site located slightly north of Lima; Bandelier's inventory for the August 24, 1892, shipment includes the Ancon material, and a note in the letter accompanying the inventory suggests that the doll that is number 4 in the checklist was almost an afterthought: "There are also a few small dolls, made by Indians of to-day, which I did not detach, although they are modern."[162]

The Myron I. Granger Archaeological Expedition to Peru, 1930

Between January and July 1930, Ronald Leroy Olson, then curator of South American archaeology at the AMNH, conducted fieldwork in Peru and Ecuador. The expedition was named for its sponsor, Myron Granger, and was specifically dedicated to improving the museum's South American collections.[163] Although Olson had no previous experience in South America,[164] he conducted excavations during that fieldwork at several sites along the coast of Peru and obtained the archaeological bags that are numbers 7 and 8 in the checklist. Unfortunately, other than the attribution to the Nazca Valley in southern Peru, contextual data for these specific pieces are minimal.[165]

However, the collection of archaeological material gathered by Olson is accompanied by a rich visual ethnographic data set. The Museum of Science and Industry in Chicago contributed $500 to Olson's trip for a collection of weaving implements and a study of textiles.[166] Consequently, the expedition archive includes photographs of weavers (male and female) taken by Olson in highland Peru and in Ecuador (fig. 62).[167] He also made a short silent film entitled *Weavers of the Andean Highlands*. The movie documents textile production in a range of contexts; in addition to domestic settings, the film includes scenes showing prisoners weaving belts and shawls to exchange for food and coca leaves.[168]

La Prensa Expedition to Q'ero, Peru, 1955

In 1955 an expedition of Peruvian scholars set out to Q'ero in the Department of Cuzco, Peru.[169] The village of Q'ero is notoriously remote, located approximately one hundred miles east of the city of Cuzco, and it takes two days to travel there by foot or on horseback from the nearest road. Led by Dr. Oscar Nuñez del Prado Castro, an anthropologist at the Universidad Nacional de San Abad del Cusco, the 1955 team included geographers, archaeologists, and folklorists. The Peruvian newspaper *La Prensa*, which sponsored the expedition, covered it extensively in articles that emphasize Q'ero's isolation. Written under such headlines as "Living Museum from Inca Times Studied by Peruvian Scientists,"[170] the newspaper's accounts adopt patriotic overtones, expressing pride in both Peru's "Inca" history and its modern research team.[171] The AMNH's involvement with the expedition to Q'ero appears to have been facilitated through personal connections. *La Prensa*'s owner, Pedro Gerado Beltrán-Espantoso, was married to an American woman, who was friendly with Harry Tschopik, then assistant curator of ethnology at the AMNH, and she liaised with Nuñez del Prado "to gather a representative ethnological collection for the American Museum of Natural History during his expedition to Q'ero."[172] It was left to "Dr. Nuñez del Prado's good judgment to make the proper selection,"[173] and he acquired forty-two objects for the museum at a cost of $100. Q'ero is particularly known for its distinctive weaving patterns,[174] and the forty-two pieces include ponchos, shawls, belts, and thirteen coca bags. Of these, examples 5, 22, and 23 in the checklist are exhibited in *Carrying Coca*. In addition to the newspaper clippings and accession documents, the accession file on the Beltrán Q'ero collection includes several photographs taken by the expedition team, including an image of two men with *phukucho*, coca bags made from the hide of a llama or alpaca (fig. 63). The Q'ero archive includes details on some of the motifs woven into the accessioned textiles, as well as some supplementary notes on who within the community would have used or worn particular types of textiles.

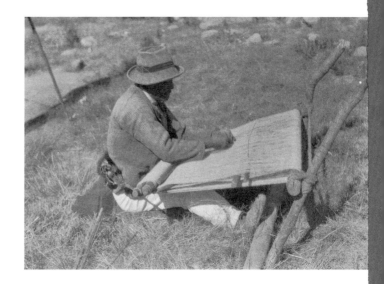

Fig. 62 (right). Ronald Olson. Male weaver in Quito, Ecuador, 1930. Image 274106, American Museum of Natural History Library.

Fig. 63 (below). Men chewing coca from *phukucho* (fur coca bag) in Q'ero, Department of Cuzco, Peru, 1955. Courtesy of the Division of Anthropology, American Museum of Natural History.

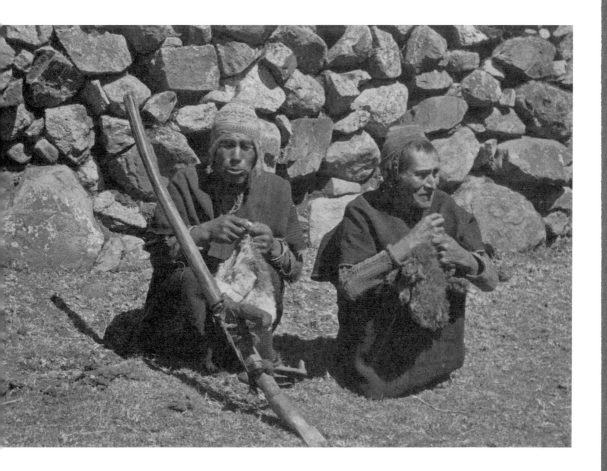

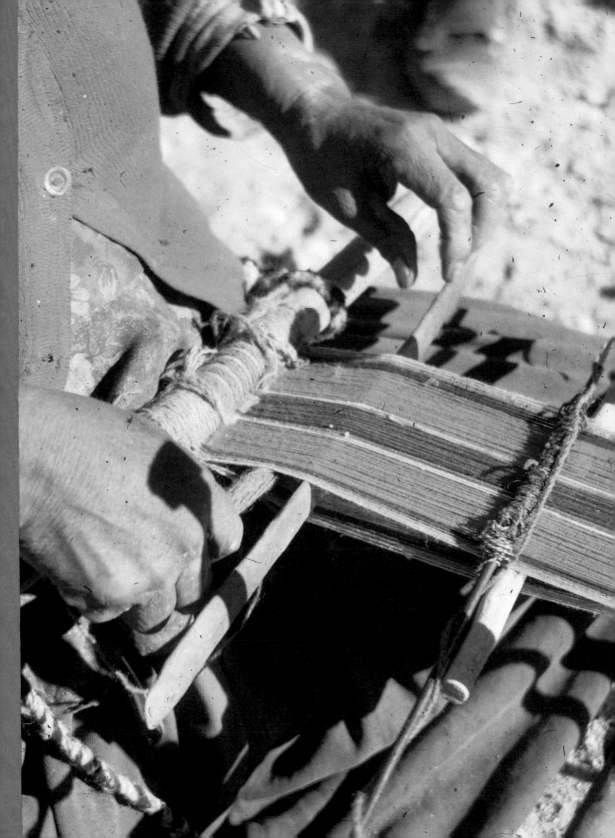

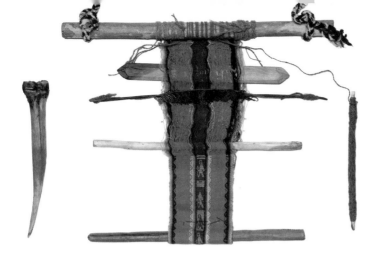

The Grace Goodell Collection, 1968

Five of the coca bags in this exhibition (cats. 3, 27, 28, 29, and 30) are ethnographic bags collected in 1968. Junius B. Bird, the curator of South American archaeology at the AMNH during the mid-twentieth century, had a particular interest in textiles,[175] and it was during Bird's tenure that the museum sponsored an expedition to collect ethnographic textiles from the Andes. The expedition was conducted by Grace Goodell, who later earned a doctorate in anthropology from Columbia University and went on to become a leading scholar in international development.

The collection is notable not only for the range of pieces collected, but also for the diligent and detailed documentation that accompanies it. In her twenties at the time of the expedition, Goodell spent several months working with weavers in various communities in Bolivia; she recorded the community from which every piece was acquired and, in a few cases, the name of the weaver who produced it. Reflecting her interest in understanding process and technologies, the Goodell collection also includes weaving tools and unfinished textiles still on the loom (e.g., cat. 18). The collection is made even richer by color slides that Goodell took in order to record finished textiles, as well as people making and wearing them. Her attention to record keeping in the field has enabled scholars to match images of textiles being woven in Bolivia forty-five years ago with the actual objects in the collection (figs. 64, 65).

Fig. 64 (opposite). Grace Goodell. Coca bag, being woven in Oruro, Bolivia, 1968. Courtesy of the Division of Anthropology, American Museum of Natural History.

Fig. 65. Coca bag in the process of being woven. Yarn, cotton, wool; double-faced float-warp pattern and plain weave. Courtesy of the Division of Anthropology, American Museum of Natural History, 40.1/3535.

Notes

1 The two most extensively spoken indigenous languages in the Andes are Quechua and Aymara. *Chuspa* is the Quechua word for a coca bag, and for the sake of clarity I have used it throughout much of this essay. The Aymara word for a coca bag is *huallqepo*.

2 In this respect, this essay is theoretically guided by scholarly discourse that concentrates on the social significance of craft objects. This focus conceives of material culture as both reflective and constitutive of human behavior, social relationships, and cultural identities. The published literature adopting this approach is vast and is represented by various academic disciplines, although it has been particularly popular among anthropological archaeologists. See, among others, Appadurai, ed., *The Social Life of Things*; Childe, *Man Makes Himself*; Chilton, ed., *Material Meanings*; Hodder, ed., *The Archaeology of Contextual Meanings*; Hodder, *The Meaning of Things*; and Hurcombe, *Archaeological Artifacts as Material Culture*.

3 These include both published and unpublished collections. In this essay I have relied heavily on analyses of collections at the American Museum of Natural History, the Brooklyn Museum, the British Museum, and the Museo Contisuyo in Peru.

4 The ethnographic data on textiles were principally gathered by myself and Ryan Williams, with the assistance of students from the University of Illinois at Chicago, under the auspices of an ethnographic collections project sponsored by the Field Museum of Natural History in Chicago entitled "Ceramic and Textile Arts of the Descendants of the Incas." The project ran from 2007 to 2009, and it was followed up by subsequent conversations I had with weavers in 2010 and 2013. The research was undertaken in the Cuzco and Moquegua Valleys in Peru. The discussions of coca are influenced by the observations and conversations I have had in Bolivia and southern Peru, beginning in 2001. Gathered in particular moments and places and read through the lens of informant and ethnographer, these ethnographic details should be understood as specific and not general.

5 Moseley, *The Incas and Their Ancestors*, 22–23.

6 Silverman, "Touring Ancient Times," 881–902. Archaeological tourism is especially significant to the economy in Peru, where the most famous Inca site, Machu Picchu, is located.

7 Llamas and alpacas are both domesticated camelids. Llamas are bigger and stronger than alpacas and are commonly used as pack animals. Their hair is coarser and greasier than alpaca fiber, which is softer and longer. Because of its strength, weavers braid spun llama fiber into slings and ropes or weave it into utilitarian sacks, but weavers and wearers alike prefer alpaca fiber for clothing and accessories. Vicuña and guanaco are both wild camelids. Vicuña wool is extremely soft and sought after for global as well as Andean textile production. The species is endangered, and the export of vicuña wool was banned for a period, although it has now resumed. The species of cotton that grows most extensively in Andean South America is *Gossypium barbadense*. It was domesticated in the Andes during the Late Pre-Ceramic Period (3000–1800 BC).

8 Wallert and Boytner, "Dyes from the Tumilaca and Chiribaya Cultures," 853–61.

9 Several weaving techniques utilized in the Andes are unknown elsewhere. Techniques that distinguish Andean weaving include discontinuous warp-and weft-patterning and specific structures of complementary warp weaves, as well as some unusual braiding types and other non-loom techniques. Rowe, "The Art of Peruvian Textiles," 330.

10 Jolie et al., "Cordage, Textiles, and the Andean Pleistocene Peopling of the Andes," 287. Plants used in the antecedents of modern Andean weaving include Tillandsia, a bromeliad, and Furcraea, a type of agave. Feltham, *Peruvian Textiles*, 18.

11 Bird, "Pre-Ceramic Art from Huaca Prieta," 30; Bird et al., *The Preceramic Excavations at the Huaca Prieta*, 194.

12 Frame, "What the Women Were Wearing," 13–53; Paul, *Paracas Ritual Attire*.

13 Bergh, "Tapestry-woven Tunics"; Conklin, "Pucara and Tiahuanaco Tapestry," 1–44.

14 "Fine clothing was just as common as that of the most frequent offerings. It was a part of nearly every major sacrifice. Clothing was made for this purpose with certain ceremonies and in different ways. Part of it was men's garments and part of it was women's garments. Some of the garments were large, some small. They dressed the idols and dead bodies of the lords in his clothing, and put alongside them folded garments. Thus, not counting the garment that each idol already had, they put another folded garment next to it. However, the amount of clothing that was burned was so much greater that there was no comparison." Cobo, *Inca Religion and Customs*, 117.

15 Costin, "Housewives, Chosen Women, Skilled Men," 123; Murra, *The Economic Organization of the Inca State*, 66.

16 Essentially "chosen women," aqllakuna are often compared by scholars to Rome's vestal virgins.

17 Phipps, "Garments and Identity in the Colonial Andes," 26.

18 Pre-Hispanic garment forms were not completely discarded in the Colonial Period. In several communities in southern Peru, women continue to weave and wear "Inca"–style wrapped dresses for special occasions. Roel Mendizabal and Borja Chavez, *Anaco de Camilaca*.

19 Ackerman, "Clothes and Identity in the Central Andes," 231–60; Femenias, *Gender and the Boundaries of Dress in Contemporary Peru*, 299; Oakland Rodman, "Textiles and Ethnicity," 316–40.

20 Even weaving communities that own herds of llamas and alpacas are affected by this problem. In the Carumas Valley of Peru, families used to weave textiles from their own herds of alpaca. However, in the past ten to fifteen years, more and more owners have sold all their camelid fiber to dealers in Puno and instead purchased synthetic threads for weaving.

21 Some older weavers in southern Peru express their disdain for these colors by referring to them as "scandalous."

22 Femenias, "Regional Dress of the Colca Valley," 179–204; Healy, *Llamas, Weavings and Organic Chocolate*, 267–89; Meisch, "We Are Sons of Atahualpa," 145–77; Zorn, *Weaving a Future*.

23 Barraza Lescano, "Acllas y Personajes Emplumados."

24 The identification of the individual as elite is based on the large ear spools he is wearing.

25 Guaman Poma de Ayala, *The First New Chronicle and Good Government*.

26 Bertonio, *Vocabulario de la Lengua Aymara*, 96. Early Quechua dictionaries also list 'istalla, glossed as ystilla in Spanish, for women's coca bags. Rowe, "Inca Weaving and Costume," 30. In the Quechua–speaking village of Ichunya in southern Peru, coca bags are today only worn by men, and the word ystilla is currently used to describe a small bag that is not used for coca. Fermina Flores Ticona, conversation with author, July 17, 2013.

27 Cobo, *Inca Religion and Customs*, 185.

28 Markham, *Travels in Peru and India*, 237.

29 Heckman, *Woven Stories*, 86.

30 Having cleaned the fiber, the weaver teases it out gently, twisting a small length to attach to the spindle. By rubbing the tips of the spindle between her fingers or hands, she sets it into a spin before dropping it. As the spindle continues to twirl, she draws the fibers out by hand and they

are twisted into yarn. The direction in which yarn is twisted is referred to as a Z or S, reflecting the alignment of fibers in a thread. As a weaver works through her bundle of fiber, she wraps the spun thread around the spindle. Plied fibers are twisted in the opposite direction to that in which they were spun. In the southern Andes, yarn is typically Z-spun and S-plied, and yarn crafted in the opposite arrangement (S-spun and Z-plied) has long been associated with witchcraft and healing. Rowe and Cohen, *Hidden Threads of Peru*, 84; La Barre, *The Aymara Indians of the Lake Titicaca Plateau*, 107.

31 Spinning requires much more time than weaving. In the Andes, people often use portable spindles in tandem with other activities, such as walking long distances or tending herds. Rowe, "The Art of Peruvian Textiles," 329.

32 Oakland Rodman, "Weaving in a High Land," 22.

33 Horizontal four-stake ground looms are held in place by four posts inserted vertically into the ground. A horizontal bar, called a loom bar, is attached to the posts at each end. The warp is the first set of threads used in weaving and is created by continuously wrapping a length of yarn in a figure-eight around the two loom bars. Although *chuspas* are small enough that a weaver can undertake this alone, for larger textiles she will require help warping the loom, and she and her assistant toss the ball of yarn back and forth between the loom bars, both of them making sure that the warp threads are evenly spaced.

34 Perpendicular to the warp threads, the weft threads are passed through the gap (the shed) between warp yarns and thus run the width of the cloth. In the Andes, weavers wrap weft threads around a simple stick (shuttle) to facilitate passing them through the shed. Phipps, *Looking at Textiles*, 86.

35 With plain weave, a structure is created in which the weft passes over and under alternating warp threads as it passes in one direction (e.g., from right to left). During the following passage (i.e., from left to right), the process is reversed. Thus the warps that are beneath the weft in one direction are then above it in the opposite direction. The weaver achieves this reversal by raising and lowering alternate warp threads, using a heddle rod attached to alternate warp yarns.

36 "Warp-faced" means that the warp threads are more numerous and more closely spaced than weft yarns, so that they predominate visually.

37 These weft threads are "discontinuous"; they do not pass across the entire width of the cloth but turn back on themselves to create blocks of color. This creates boundaries between wefts, which are sometimes visible as slits in the cloth. Open slits do weaken the structure of the cloth, and may be avoided using various techniques, including by linking wefts in a process called interlocking or dovetailing, when different wefts wrap around the same warp thread. Feltham, *Peruvian Textiles*, 25.

38 As the weft passes over the warp of one color, it passes under the reciprocal or complementary warp of the other color, resulting in a double faced cloth in which colors are in reverse on each face. Rowe and Cohen, *Hidden Threads of Peru*, 92.

39 Feltham, *Peruvian Textiles*, 34.

40 Rowe and Cohen, *Hidden Threads of Peru*, 102.

41 Ibid., 101.

42 Bags, although not coca bags, appear very early in the textile record. Excavators recovered fragments of net bags made from twined fiber from Guitarrero Cave in the highlands of Peru, one of the oldest archaeological sites in South America. Excavated from archaeological deposits radiocarbon dated between 12,100 and 11,000 years ago, these fragments are contemporaneous with the earliest human inhabitants of the Andes. The next oldest textile assemblages are from the small village site of Paloma on the coast of Peru. Dating to between 5900 and 3300 BC, they include simple, twined bags. Archaeologists excavated more than thirty looped bags from Huaca Prieta, a site dating to 3000–1800 BC, which was excavated during fieldwork sponsored by the AMNH in the 1940s. Adavasio and Lynch, "Preceramic Textiles and Cordage," 85; Bird et al., *The Preceramic Excavations at the Huaca Prieta*; Jolie et al., "Cordage, Textiles, and the Late Pleistocene Peopling of the Andes," 287; Vallejos, "Analisis y tipologia de los textiles de Paloma," 6–37.

43 Adelson and Tracht, *Aymara Weavings,* 124; Kroeber and Collier, *The Archaeology and Pottery of Nazca, Peru,* 68.

44 The most extensive work on *chuspas* concerns coca bags from the north coast of Chile, where the excellent preservation produced by the extremely arid Atacama Desert means that there is a continuous record of textile objects from 7000 BC on. The north Chilean coca bag literature has focused on identifying the differences between local traditions and *chuspa* styles brought with Inca conquest in AD 1470. Carmona Sciaraffia, "Los Nuevos Patrones Formales y Decorativos," 26–27; Horta and Aguero, "Definicion de Chuspa,"48.

45 Paracas textiles constitute one of the most elaborate traditions in the pre-Hispanic Andes. Textiles largely come from burials found in the Paracas Peninsula, 155 miles south of Lima. The Paracas dead were placed in baskets and wrapped in layer upon layer of cloth, which is particularly famous for labor intensive polychrome embroidery that depicted anthropomorphized figures, serpents, and winged creatures. The sheer quantity of well-preserved textiles has enabled scholars to reconstruct the ceremonial wardrobe of Paracas leaders. Scholars have identified a diverse range of Paracas textile forms, but intriguingly coca bags appear to be missing from these assemblages. In her 1941 analysis of Paracas embroideries in museum collections, Stafford refers to two coca bags in the Brooklyn Museum. However, Anne Paul has questioned this identification, since she found none in her extensive analyses of Paracas materials at the Museo Nacional de Antropologia y Arqueologia in Lima. Paul also notes that no reference was made to coca bags when the Paracas mummy bundles were first unwrapped. Paul, *Paracas Ritual Attire,* 47; Stafford, *Paracas Embroideries,* 90.

46 Accession records for 30.1215, Brooklyn Museum. Analysis and identification by Nobuko Kajitani and Ann Rowe in 1993.

47 Although Moche sites are coastal, textiles are not well preserved because the north coast of Peru endures periodic heavy rains and the soil there is considerably more acidic than in the south of the country.

48 Although well known from depictions, the scene was long thought to represent a myth. However, during the excavation of high-status Moche tombs in 1987, individuals accompanied by huge wealth and sacrificed attendants were found buried dressed in the outfits depicted in the Presentation Scene, including the half-bird/half-human figure. Each individual has been physically found several times, and given that the image was repeatedly crafted for centuries, the figures are now interpreted as representing social roles in Moche society rather than specific persons.

49 DeMarrais et al., "Ideology, Materialization and Power Strategies," 26.

50 Horta and Aguero, "Definicion de Chuspa," 48.

51 Rowe, "Inca Weaving and Costume," 30.

52 Adelson, *Aymara Weavings,* 124.

53 Phipps et al., *The Colonial Andes,* 169.

54 Von Tschudi, *Travels in Peru,* 313.

55 Ysidora Yony Nina Jorge and Fermina Ticona Flores, conversations with author, July 17, 2013.

56 "El huallqepo es asi, no hay que cambiarlos," translated as "A coca bag is like that, there's no reason to change them." Ysidora Yony Nina Jorge, conversation with author, July 17, 2013.

57 Sánchez Gómez, class paper, Bard Graduate Center, 2013.

58 Zorn, *Weaving a Future,* 33.

59 Ysidora Yony Nina Jorge and Fermina Flores Ticona, conversations with author, July 17, 2013.

60 Cobo, *Inca Religion and Customs,* 116.

61 Although differences between types of domesticated coca were recorded as early as the 16th century, when chroniclers cited the Quechua terms *mamas* coca (a large-leafed coca that grew on the Andean slopes) and *ttupa* coca (a smaller and more flavorful leaf that was cultivated along the coast), scholars largely overlooked the morphological, geographical, and ecological differences between varieties of domesticated coca until the 1970s and 1980s. *Erythroxylum coca* var. *coca,* also known as Huánuco, Bolivian, or *ceja de montana* coca, thrives in wet montane forests and grows

most extensively on the eastern slopes of the Andes between 500 and 2,000 meters above sea level. Characterized by large, thin leaves, Huánuco coca has comparatively high cocaine content and is the variety used most extensively in illicit cocaine production. *Erythroxylum coca* var. *ipadu*, or Amazonian coca, grows in the western Amazonian basin in areas of Colombia, Brazil, and Peru. It has large leaves and considerably lower cocaine content than other cultivated cocas. Amazonian coca leaves are the only domesticated variety prepared as a powder and not chewed whole. *Erythroxylum novogranatense* var. *novogranatense*, or Colombian coca, has adapted to a hot, moist climate and grows in parts of Colombia and coastal Venezuela. Colombian coca is named for Nueva Granada, the Colonial Period name for modern Colombia. The plant has small, narrow, bright yellow-green leaves. Resistant to drought, Colombian coca is more tolerant of diverse ecological conditions than other domesticated varieties and has been successfully cultivated beyond its ancestral environment including in Sri Lanka, India, and Jamaica. *Erythroxylum novogranatense* var. *truxillense,* or Trujillo coca, is adapted to an arid coastal environment and farmers cultivate it between 200 and 1,800 meters above sea level along the coast of northern Peru and in the Upper Marañon Valley. Trujillo coca has small, brittle, light-green leaves. Trujillo coca's distinct flavor includes the essential oil of wintergreen, a feature that made it popular in 19th-century medicinal preparations of coca. It is legally exported from its namesake, the northern Peruvian city of Trujillo, to the United States, where the flavor of the leaf is extracted and used in the production of Merchandise No.5, the flavoring agent used in Coca-Cola. Gootenberg, "Secret Ingredients," 233–65; Plowman, "Botanical Perspectives on Coca," 103–17; Plowman, "The Ethnobotany of Coca"; Plowman, "The Origin, Evolution, and Diffusion of Coca"; Rostworowski de Diez Canseco, *Plantaciones Prehispanicas de Coca.*

62 Allen, *The Hold Life Has,* 221. Slope cultivation is preferable because of improved soil drainage. Plowman, "The Ethnobotany of Coca," 80.

63 Drying the leaves facilitates the rapid release of the chemical constituents. Ibid., 84.

64 Coca chewing is a predictable measure of time in areas where it is commonly practiced (Allen, *The Hold Life Has*). Raimondi refers to the word *cocada*, which he states is the distance an individual can run before the effects of his coca wears off, and by extension *la cocada* is a measure of time that lasts between 35 and 40 minutes. Raimondi, *El Peru,* vol. 1, 69.

65 In his ethnography of communities involved in producing and consuming coca leaves in northern Peru, Burchard estimated that 92 percent of families in one village in the Department of Huanuco had family members working in the tropical lowlands of the department and that 82 percent of those family members were working in coca cultivation. Burchard, "Coca y Trueque de Alimentos," 225.

66 Zorn, *Weaving a Future*, 42.

67 Bolton, "Andean Coca Chewing," 630–33; Bray and Dollery, "Coca Chewing and High-Altitude Stress," 269–82; Hanna, "Further Studies of the Effects of Coca Chewing on Exercise," 200–209; Hanna, "Responses of Quechua Indians to Coca Ingestion," 273–78; Hanna, "Coca Leaf Use in Southern Peru," 281–96; Paly et al., "Plasma Levels of Cocaine in Native Peruvian Coca Chewers," 86–89.

68 Plowman, "The Ethnobotany of Coca," 100.

69 Bray and Dollery, "Coca Chewing and High-Altitude Stress." In the Upper Moquegua Valley of Peru, coca chewers have largely replaced alkali substances with sugar. Ysidora Yony Nina Jorge, conversation with author, July 17, 2013. Although sugar is effective in sweetening the leaves, it does not increase the stimulating effect of coca as lime or baking soda does.

70 Allen, *The Hold Life Has*, 221; Hanna, "Further Studies of the Effects of Coca Chewing on Exercise," 208.

71 Body heat retention increases because of mild vasoconstriction of the human body's extremities. Allen, *The Hold Life Has*, 221; Hanna, "Responses of Quechua Indians to Coca Ingestion," 276.

72 Allen, "To Be Quechua," 157–71; Allen, *The Hold Life Has*, 22; Martindale, *Coca and Cocaine*, 11.

73 Allen, *The Hold Life Has*, 222; Gagliano, "Coca and Popular Medicine in Peru," 51; Quijada Jara, *La Coca en las Costumbres Indigenas*, 33–35.

74 Quijada Jara, *La Coca en las Costumbres Indigenas*, 39–57.

75 Allen, *The Hold Life Has*, 220.

76 Ibid., 168; Burchard, "Coca y Trueque de Alimentos," 226; Gifford and Hoggarth, *Carnival and Coca Leaf*, 73; Isbell, *To Defend Ourselves*, 119; Quijada Jara, *La Coca en las Costumbres Indigenas*, 13.

77 *Pagos* vary regionally. The descriptions here draw heavily on my observations of *pagos* and discussions with *curanderos* in the Moquegua region of southern Peru. I presented these data in a preliminary form at the annual meeting of the American Anthropological Association in 2006.

78 Also spelled *incuña*, this textile form has considerable antiquity, and archaeologists have found many examples in graves from AD 300 on, along the north coast of Chile. Adelson and Tracht, *Aymara Weavings*, 116.

79 Allen, *The Hold Life Has*, 76; Ysidora Yony Nina Jorge, conversation with author, July 17, 2013.

80 Ysidora Yony Nina Jorge, conversation with author, July 17, 2013.

81 Davidson and Ladkandi, *The Devil's Miner*. For several centuries, scholars and explorers of the Andes have noted the importance of coca to miners. Von Tschudi commented "the excavators of the mines of Cerro de Pasco throw masticated coca on hard veins of metal, in the belief that it softens the ore and renders it more easy to work. The origin of this custom is easily explained, when it is recollected that in the time of the Incas it was believed that the Coyas, or the deities of metals, rendered the mountains impenetrable if they were not propitiated by the odor of coca." Von Tschudi, *Travels in Peru*, 318.

82 Allen, *The Hold Life Has*, 22.

83 For example, Heckman, *Woven Stories*, 86.

84 Zorn, *Weaving a Future*, 77.

85 Ysidora Yony Nina Jorge and Fermina Flores Ticona, conversations with author, July 17, 2013.

86 Notes in Beltrán accession file, Anthropology Archives, AMNH.

87 Clark, "The Estuquiña Textile Tradition," 680. Clark discusses the possibility that it was during the subsequent Inca period that *chuspas* became male-specific items. Kroeber, *The Archaeology and Pottery of Nazca, Peru*, 54.

88 Adelson and Tracht, *Aymara Weavings*, 124.

89 "Altomisayoqs, the highest form of Andean ritual specialists . . . protect their coca in a *chuspa* made from the pelt of a baby alpaca, the softest of the fibers after vicuña. Their right to use the bag is a symbol of the position they have attained in life." Heckman, *Woven Stories*, 137.

90 Ibid. In an area where a *chuspa* is only carried by a man, a woman should offer coca from her *unkuña*.

91 Ibid., 71.

92 Field notes in Beltrán accession file, Anthropology Archives, AMNH.

93 Zorn, *Weaving a Future*, 76.

94 The four cultivated forms of coca are more closely related to each other than to other species of *Erythroxylum*, which suggests that they probably share common genetic stock. Because *E. coca* var. *coca* (Huánuco coca) behaves in many ways like a wild plant, it is most likely the ancestral cultivated form. Transplantation resulted in, for example, the evolution of *E. novo* var. *truxillense*, which evolved from *E. coca* in response to attempts to grow coca in more arid coastal environments about 2000 BC. Plowman, "Botanical Perspectives on Coca," 115; Plowman, "The Origin, Evolution, and Diffusion of Coca," 156.

95 Botanic remains perish unless they are in very arid areas (e.g., deserts) or in waterlogged environments (e.g., peat bogs). Fortunately for students of plants in ancient South America, the coast of Peru and northern Chile is one of the driest deserts in the world, and botanic evidence is extensive in this region near the Pacific Ocean. Renfrew and Bahn, *Archaeology*, 55.

96 The sites are Asia (1800 BC), locations in the Chillon Valley (1900–1750 BC), and Ancon (1800–1400 BC). Cohen, "Archaeological Plant Remains from the Central Coast of Peru," 23–50; Cohen Engel, "A Preceramic Settlement on the Central Coast of Peru," 1–139; Patterson, "Central Peru," 316–21.

97 Hastorf, "Archaeological Evidence of Coca," 297.

98 Cartmell et al., "The Frequency and Antiquity of Prehistoric Coca-Leaf-Chewing Practices in Northern Chile," 260–68.

99 Before modern dental hygiene practices, coca consumption resulted in caries and premature tooth loss, another excellent skeletal indicator of coca chewing in the past. Aufderheide, *The Scientific Study of Mummies*, 157; Indriati and Buikstra, "Coca Chewing in Prehistoric Coastal Peru," 243. A study claiming that dental calculus built up as a result of the lime chewed with coca leaf, and was therefore evidence of coca leaf chewing when found on archaeological skeletons, has now been persuasively challenged and dental caries are considered to be more reliable indicators. Klepinger et al., "Prehistoric Dental Calculus Gives Evidence for Coca in Early Coastal Ecuador," 506–7; Ubelaker and Stothert, "Elemental Analysis of Alkalis and Dental Deposits," 77–89.

100 Lathrap et al., *Ancient Ecuador*, 47.

101 Ibid., 48.

102 Burger and Salazar, *Machu Picchu*, 198; Korpisaari and Parssinen, *Pariti*, 118; Lumbreras and Amat, "Secuencia arqueologica del altiplano occidental del Titicaca."

103 Aufderheide, *The Scientific Study of Mummies*, 157.

104 Goldstein, *Andean Diaspora*, 214.

105 Vanstan, *Textiles from Beneath the Temple at Pachacamac, Peru*, 3.

106 Aufderheide, *The Scientific Study of Mummies*, 158.

107 Rostworowski de Diez Canseco, *Plantaciones Prehispanicas de Coca*, 251. The Inca government moved entire communities of specialists in order to congregate them to produce for the state. Migrants moved under this system were called *mitmaqkuna* and included weavers, potters, herders, miners, and coca farmers. D'Altroy, *The Incas*, 248.

108 de Molina, *Account of the Fables and Rites of the Incas*, 28. "They also paid homage to the coca bushes. They chew coca and have the coca mama [ceremony]. They kiss it and put it in their mouths." Guaman Poma de Ayala, *The First New Chronicle and Good Government*, 207.

109 Acosta, *The Natural and Moral History of the Indies*, 244; Cobo, *Inca Religion and Customs*, 116; de Molina, *Account of the Fables and Rites of the Incas*, 25; Gavilan Ramos, *Historia de Copacabana*, 145–47; Guamon Poma de Ayala, *The First New Chronicle and Good Government*, 205; Sarmiento de Gamboa, *The History of the Incas*, 146.

110 Cobo, *Inca Religion and Customs*, 116.

111 Reinhard and Ceruti, *Inca Rituals and Sacred Mountains*.

112 Bray et al., "A Compositional Analysis of Pottery Vessels," 85.

113 King, ed., *Peruvian Featherworks*, 192.

114 In the Andes, the source for spondylus shell is the coast of Ecuador. It thus represents a long-distance exchange good that was highly valued and particularly sought after for ritual occasions.

115 Gavilan Ramos, *Historia de Copacabana y de la Milagrosa Imagen de su Virgen*, 145–47.

116 Rowe, "Inca Weaving and Costume," 30.

117 For example, sandals and a *chuspa* were the insignia of an *utacaymayoc*, a mayor from the Inca heartland. Zuidema, "Hierarchy and Space in Incaic Social Organization," 68.

118 Acosta, *The Natural and Moral History of the Indies*, 246; Finley Hughes, "Weaving Imperial Ideas," 156; Mariani, *Coca and its Therapeutic Application*, 19.

119 Murra, "Notes on Pre-Columbian Cultivation of Coca Leaf," 51.

120 Finley Hughes, "Weaving Imperial Ideas," 170.

121 Gagliano, "The Coca Debate in Colonial Peru," 44–47.

122 Garcilaso de la Vega and Guaman Poma de Ayala were both authors of Andean descent, and their accounts of Inca life generally present a more favorable take on Andean practices than many other chroniclers, although in the case of coca, Guaman Poma took a decidedly negative view.

123 Cobo, *Inca Religion and Customs*, 169.

124 Guaman Poma de Ayala, *The First New Chronicle and Good Government*, 214.

125 Allen, *The Hold Life Has*, 220; Gagliano, "The Coca Debate in Colonial Peru," 44.

126 In 1545 silver was discovered in the mines at Potosi, in Bolivia. The city was for a short time the wealthiest in the New World. The mercury necessary for producing high-grade silver was mined in Huancavelica (in modern Peru). The dangers and sickness attendant with forced labor in the mines were significant factors in the massive population decline in the Andes during the early Colonial Period. D'Altroy, *The Incas*, 320–21.

127 In 1553 Pedro Cieza de Leon commented that "Anyone holding an *encomienda* [estate] of Indians considered his main crop the number of baskets of coca he gathered." Cieza de Leon, *The Incas*, 260. In 1572 Pedro Sarmiento de Gamboa recounted that "there was a knight, a citizen of Cuzco named Don Luis Palomino who, having given as a present (Dona Mayor Palomino his sister being a maiden) a very handsome harpsichord, this cavalier gave in return 2000 cestos [baskets] of coca placed in Potosi, at a time when coca was worth $12 to $14 the cesto. For this soldier rose from great poverty, but went back to Castille very rich and influential." Sarmiento de Gamboa, *The History of the Incas*, 233.

128 Allen, *The Hold Life Has*, 220.

129 Others in turn criticized the working conditions of the coca plantations, a charge addressed by reforms under the Second Marques of Canete (1555–60) that sought to improve working conditions in the coca fields and reduce coca cultivation. Gagliano, "The Coca Debate in Colonial Peru,"47.

130 Von Tschudi, *Travels in Peru*, 315.

131 Presta, "Undressing the Coya and Dressing the Indian Woman," 67.

132 Von Tschudi wrote in 1854 that "the moderate use of coca is not merely not innoxious, but . . . it may be even very conducive to health" and listed its effects in suppressing hunger and fatigue, and curing minor ailments." Von Tschudi, *Travels in Peru*, 316. Clements Markham, who was in South America to collect Chinchona plants and seeds for their introduction into India, also recorded his observations on the coca leaf and commented that "the coca leaf is the great source of comfort and enjoyment to the Peruvian Indian. . . . [I]ts use produces invigorating effects which are not possessed by the other stimulants." Markham, *Travels in Peru and India*, 232.

133 Cited in Mariani, *Coca and its Therapeutic Application*, 30.

134 Gagliano, "Coca and Popular Medicine in Peru," 58.

135 Gootenberg, "Cocaine in Chains," 324; Karch, *A Brief History of Cocaine*, 48.

136 Gootenberg, "Cocaine in Chains," 325.

137 Mariani, *Coca and its Therapeutic Application*, 60.

138 Karch, *A Brief History of Cocaine*, 25.

139 Gootenberg, "Secret Ingredients," 235. Article 27.1 of the 1961 U.N. Single Convention on Narcotic Drugs, the convention that declared coca leaf production should cease within 25 years, states that signatory parties "may permit the use of coca leaves for the preparation of a flavouring agent, which shall not contain any alkaloids, and, to the extent necessary for such use, may permit the production, import, export, trade in and possession of such leaves." See Gootenberg, "Secret Ingredients," for a detailed discussion of the role of U.S. commercial interests in the formulation of national and international drug policy.

140 Gootenberg, "Cocaine in Chains," 328.

141 Most notable of coca supporters in the early 20th century was W. Golden Mortimer, a physician whose monumental and immensely detailed 1901 volume on coca refers to it as "The Divine Plant of the Incas." Mortimer, *History of Coca*.

142 Gootenberg, "Between Coca and Cocaine," 129; Gootenberg, "Cocaine in Chains," 238.

143 Caceres Santa Maria, "Historia, Prejucios y Version Psiquiatrica del Coqueo Andino," 32.

144 Gutierrez-Noriega and von Hagen, "Coca," 148.

145 These include Sergio Quijada Jara's short book *La Coca en las Costumbres Indigenas*, in which he documents Quechua songs and refrains about coca as well as cultural practices. Efforts to document and demonstrate the importance of coca leaves in the Andes have continued. Published in 1986, Carter and Mamani's volume is an often-cited detailed account of coca in Bolivian communities. Carter and Mamani, *Coca en Bolivia.*

146 United Nations Office on Drugs and Crime, *Single Convention on Narcotic Drugs.*

147 Demarest, "Cocaine: Middle Class High"; Kay, "Violent Opportunities," 97–127; Keefe, "Cocaine Incorporated"; Kernaghan, *Coca's Gone.*

148 During a conference on coca and cocaine in Andean nations in the mid-1980s, John T. Cusack, chief of staff of the U.S. House of Representatives Select Committee on Narcotics Control and Abuse, adopted moral overtones when he asserted that coca-producing countries had "an obligation to phase out coca chewing and the coca that is being produced for chewing. And secondly, their main obligation to every nation in the world, particularly the developed nations that are most severely affected by cocaine, is to bring under control, in their territory, the unlicensed and illicit production of coca leaf." Cusack, "The International Narcotics Control System," 70.

149 Farthing, "Social Impacts Associated with Antidrug Law 1008," 235–70; Pacini and Franquemont, *Coca and Cocaine.* The impacts vary depending on an individual country's particular coca history. Coca chewing was eliminated in Ecuador in the 19th century, and thus the effects of recent international narcotic legislation are less severe than in Bolivia and Peru.

150 Allen, *The Hold Life Has*, 227.

151 Sanabria, "The Discourse and Practice of Repression and Resistance in the Chapare," 169–94; Spedding, "Cocataki, Taki-Coca," 117–38.

152 Landes, *Cocalero.*

153 The U.S. objected to this reservation, but of the 61 countries required to veto it, only 15 (among them the U.S., the U.K., and Mexico) opposed it.

154 These pockets are called *nuñu* (breast) in Quechua.

155 Femenias, "Regional Dress of the Colca Valley, Peru," 179.

156 Ysidora Yony Nina Jorge, conversation with author, July 17, 2013.

157 Fermina Flores Ticona, conversation with author, July 17, 2013.

158 Ysidora Yony Nina Jorge, conversation with author, July 17, 2013.

159 Allen, *The Hold Life Has,* 34.

160 Among the most famous are excavations conducted by Junius B. Bird (curator of South American archaeology at the AMNH from 1939 to 1973) at very early archaeological sites in Chile in the 1930s and by Craig Morris (Bird's successor and curator of South American archaeology from 1975 to 2006) at the enormous Inca site of Huánuco Pampa in the 1970s.

161 Freed, *Anthropology Unmasked*, vol. 2, 864.

162 Bandelier inventory, dated August 24, 1892, Anthropology Archives, AMNH.

163 It had been 27 years since the AMNH had sponsored research in the Andes and the curator in chief Clark Wissler considered South America a research priority. Wissler championed Olson's appointment and tried to retain him on staff when Olson was offered a job at the University of Washington. Freed, *Anthropology Unmasked*, 872.

164 This was to be Olson's one and only field season in the Andes. His letters to Wissler from the field indicate considerable frustration with the politics of archaeological fieldwork in Peru, and a year after returning from the Granger expedition, he resigned from his post at the AMNH to accept a position as associate professor of anthropology at the University of California, Berkeley, where he returned to his earlier North American research focused on the Northwest Coast. Granger Expedition, Olson file, Anthropology Archives, AMNH.

165 Pickman, class paper, Bard Graduate Center, 2013.

166 Freed, *Anthropology Unmasked*, vol. 2, 872.

167 Granger expedition to Peru, special collections, AMNH Library.

168 Film 288, AMNH Library. The film notes that outside the prison, weaving is women's work, but that it constitutes an important source of income for men in jail. Today in the community of Mahuay-pampa, Department of Cuzco, Peru, simple motifs are referred to as "jail designs" (*diseños del carcel*) because although weaving is a female activity in Mahuaypampa, men who serve time in prison often learn to weave simple blankets with relatively easy designs.

169 Q'ero has been the subject of considerable research since the *La Prensa* expedition, much of it focused on textiles. Steven Webster, an anthropologist who worked in Q'ero during the 1960s and 1970s, documented a ceremony there conducted in honor of textiles. Rowe and Cohen, *Hidden Threads of Peru*, 14. John Cohen, a photographer, filmmaker, and musician, made numerous trips to Q'ero during the second half of the twentieth century and produced a series of short films on daily life and ritual practice in the community. Cohen also collected textiles there and donated 57 of these to the AMNH. A sample of cotton with seeds (40.1/2235) collected by Cohen in Q'ero is exhibited in *Carrying Coca*.

170 Sánchez Gómez, class paper, Bard Graduate Center, 2013.

171 The members of the research team were all Peruvian, apart from an American photographer, Malcolm Burke, who was profiled in the newspaper. *La Prensa* (Lima), August 28, 1955.

172 Letter from Miriam Beltrán to Miss Bella Weitzner at AMNH, dated July 11, 1955. Anthropology Archives, AMNH.

173 Ibid.

174 Q'ero's textiles are recognizable for the warp-patterned bands decorated with *ch'unchu* (dancers from the jungle) and *inti* (sun) motifs. Q'ero textiles are also notable because men still wear pre-Hispanic style tunics. Rowe and Cohen, *Hidden Threads of Peru*, 14.

175 During field work in 1946–47 at the Late Pre-Ceramic Period (3000–1800 BC) site of Huaca Prieta in the Chicama Valley on the north coast of Peru, Bird excavated the earliest-known decorated textiles in the Andes. His interest in textile technologies continued throughout his career and he was regarded as an authority on archaeological textiles from South America. Rexer and Klein, *American Museum of Natural History*, 159.

Checklist of the Exhibition

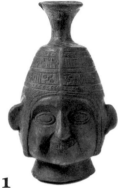

1
Jar with depiction of human face chewing coca
Chimu/Inca, Peru
AD 1100–1470
Clay; incised
6 ½ x 5 ½ x 8 in. (16.4 x 13.8 x 20.1 cm)
American Museum of Natural History, B/8875

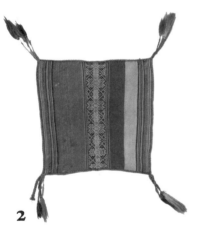

2
Carrying cloth
Vicinity of Lake Titicaca, Bolivia
20th century
Wool; warp-patterned stripes, tubular edging
with tassels
17 ¾ x 12 ¼ in. (45 x 31 cm)
Collected by Junius B. Bird, 1933, gift of
Margaret Bird, accessioned 1983
American Museum of Natural History, 40.1/5103

3
Coca bag with strap and hand-woven edge bindings
Ayata, Bolivia
20th century
Wool; single-faced warp-patterned stripes, plain-
weave stripes, single-faced warp-patterned strap
21 ¼ x 13 ⅜ in. (54 x 34 cm)
Collected by Grace Goodell, accessioned 1969
American Museum of Natural History, 40.1/3582
See fig. 25.

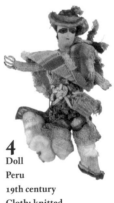

4
Doll
Peru
19th century
Cloth; knitted
4 ¾ x 2 ¾ in. (11.9 x 6.9 cm)
Collected by Adolph Bandelier, accessioned 1894
American Museum of Natural History, B/4129c

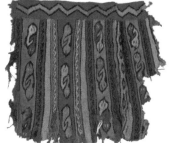

7

Bag fragment
Nazca Valley, Peru
100 BC–AD 700
Camelid fiber; weft-faced plain weave, slit tapestry
weft patterning, needlework edges
5 ⅞ x 5 ½ in. (15 x 14 cm)
Collected by Ronald Olson during the Myron Granger
Expedition, accessioned 1930
American Museum of Natural History, 41.0/5415

8

Two bags tied together
Nazca Valley, Peru
100 BC–AD 700
Camelid fiber, cotton; double-faced tapestry with
eccentric wefts, plied and beaded fringes, braided strap
Large bag: 45 ¼ x 5 ½ in. (114.9 x 14 cm);
small bag: 3 ¾ x 3 ¾ in. (9.5 x 9.5 cm)
Collected by Ronald Olson during the
Myron Granger Expedition, accessioned 1930
American Museum of Natural History, 41.0/5461
See fig. 26.

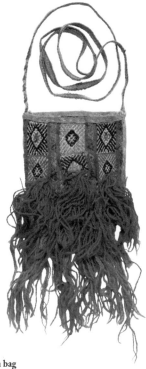

5

Coca bag
Q'ero Village, Department of Cuzco, Peru
Wool; three-warp-patterned stripes with *inti* motifs
35 ⅜ x 7 ½ in. (90 x 19 cm)
Collected during *La Prensa*–sponsored expedition to
Q'ero, accessioned 1956
American Museum of Natural History, 40.0/8907
See page 4.

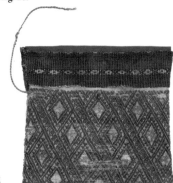

9

Bag
Peru
Pre-Hispanic
Camelid fiber, cotton; plain weave, single-faced
supplementary weft patterning, overcasting stitches
8 ¼ x 9 ½ in. (21 x 24 cm)
Purchased from Joseph L. Costa, accessioned 1955
American Museum of Natural History, 41.2/797

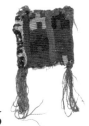

6

Miniature bag
Ancon, Peru
Pre-Hispanic
Wool; warp-faced plain weave
2 x 3 ½ in. (5 x 9 cm)
Collected by Adolph Bandelier, accessioned 1894
American Museum of Natural History, B/4728c

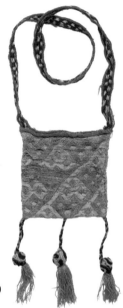

12

Alpaca fiber sample
South America
20th century
3 ⅛ x 4 in. (8 x 10 cm)
American Museum of Natural History, SAT/1261

13

Cotton with seeds
Q'ero Village, Department of Cuzco, Peru
20th century
6 ¾ x 4 in. (17 x 10 cm)
Collected by John Cohen, accessioned 1957
American Museum of Natural History, 40.1/2235

10

Bag
Chancay, Central Coast of Peru
AD 1000–1476
Camelid fiber, cotton; complementary weft patterning,
braiding, chain stitch embroidery, plied fringe
4 ⅞ x 5 ⅛ in. (12.5 x 13 cm)
Gift of the Ernest Erickson Foundation Inc., accessioned 1988
American Museum of Natural History, 41.2/8974

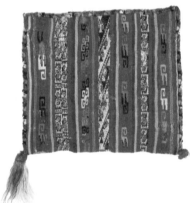

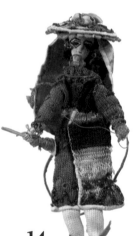

11

Bag
Inca, Ancon, Peru
1450–1532
Camelid fiber, cotton; weft-faced plain weave,
double-faced slit tapestry, cross loop stitched edging
10 ¼ x 9 ¾ in. (25.8 x 24.6 cm)
Collected by Adolph Bandelier, accessioned 1894
American Museum of Natural History, B/9647

14

Doll
Peru
19th century
Cloth, satin, bead, metal, wood; knitted
5 ⅛ x 2 ¾ in. (13 x 7 cm)
Gift of Albert C. Muller, accessioned 1970
American Museum of Natural History, 40.1/3694

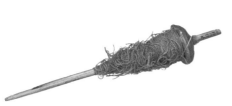

15

Spindle whorl with wool
Lima, Peru
20th century
Wood, wool
11 x 1⅝ in. (28 x 4 cm)
Gift of Margaret Bird, accessioned 1983
American Museum of Natural History 40.1/6547

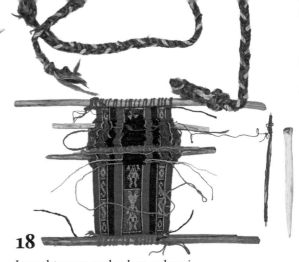

18

Incomplete woven coca bag, loom, and *ruqui*
(bone weaving tool)
Oruro, Bolivia
20th century
Wood, camelid bone, wool; double-faced warp-
float patterned stripes, plain weave
Bag: 9 x 5 ¼ in. (23 x 13.5 cm)
Collected by Grace Goodell, accessioned 1969
American Museum of Natural History, 40.1/3539
A-H, J-K

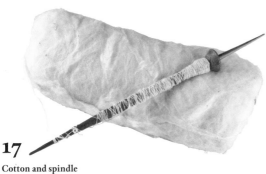

16

Spindle and whorl with spun vicuña wool
Puno, Peru
19th century
Wood, clay, vicuña thread
7 ½ x 1 ⅝ in. (19 x 4 cm)
Gift of E. P. Mathewson, accessioned 1901
American Museum of Natural History, B/9548

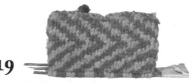

19

Incomplete knitted coca bag
Hacienda Vicos, Ancash, Peru
20th century
Wool, metal; knitted
6 ¾ x 2 ¾ x 2⅜ in. (17 x 7 x 6 cm)
Collected by William Mangin, accessioned 1953
American Museum of Natural History, 40.0/8488

17

Cotton and spindle
Bellavista, Peru
20th century
Wood, cotton fiber
Spindle: 11 x 1 ⅛ x ¾ in. (28 x 3 x 2 cm);
cotton: 9 ½ x 5 ⅛ x 4 in. (24 x 13 x 10 cm)
Gift of Margaret Bird, accessioned 1983
American Museum of Natural History, 40.1/6544

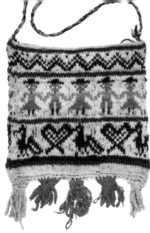

20

Bag
Highland Peru
20th century
Wool; knitted
18 ½ x 6 ½ in. (47 x 16.5 cm)
Purchased from Frank Kuhne, accessioned 1950
American Museum of Natural History, 40.0/8151

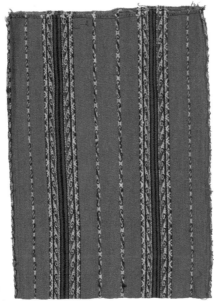

21

Coca bag
Southern Peru
20th century
Wool; hand-woven, machine-stitched along sides
16 ½ x 11 ¾ in. (42 x 30 cm)
Exchange with Grace Line Company,
accessioned 1960
American Museum of Natural History, 40.1/707

22

Phukucho bag
Q'ero Village, Department of Cuzco, Peru
20th century
Llama hide, fur
15 x 8 ⅝ in. (38 x 22 cm)
Collected during *La Prensa*–sponsored
expedition to Q'ero, accessioned 1956
American Museum of Natural History, 40.0/8913
See fig. 46.

23

Coca bag
Q'ero Village, Department of Cuzco, Peru
20th century
Vicuña wool; central warp-patterned stripe with
inti motifs, warp stripe at selvage, fringed
37 ⅜ x 6 ¼ in. (95 x 16 cm)
Collected during *La Prensa*–sponsored
expedition to Q'ero, accessioned 1956
American Museum of Natural History, 40.0/8906
See fig. 34.

24

Bag
Central Coast, Peru
AD 1100–1532
Camelid fiber, cotton; weft-faced plain weave, slit
tapestry, running overcasting stitches, braiding
15 ¾ x 5 ½ in. (40 x 14 cm)
Gift of Mr. Frederick Landmann,
accessioned 1979
American Museum of Natural History, 41.2/7683
See fig. 23.

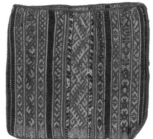

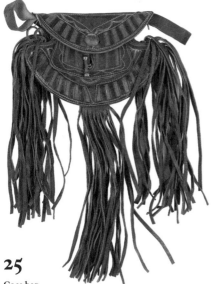

25

Coca bag
La Paz, Bolivia
20th century
Leather, metal, pigment, thread
11 ¾ x 8 ⅝ in. (30 x 22 cm)
Gift of Professor Robert Peele, accessioned 1937
American Museum of Natural History, 40.0/4932

26

Bag with carrying strap
Island of Taquile, Peru
20th century
Wool; warp-faced plain weave, complementary
warp-weave warp-patterned strap; edge binding
of two-strand twining
30 ¾ x 13 ⅜ in. (78 x 34 cm)
Gift of Mrs. Harry Tschopik, accessioned 1955
American Museum of Natural History, 40.0/8870
See fig. 24.

27

Coca bag
Oruro, Bolivia
20th century
Wool; double-faced warp pattern
9 ⅞ x 9 ½ in. (25 x 24 cm)
Collected by Grace Goodell, accessioned 1969
American Museum of Natural History, 40.1/3537

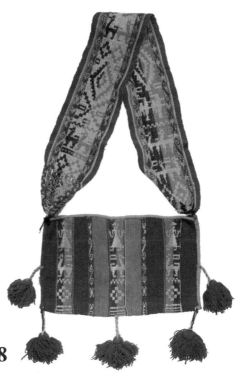

28

Coca bag with strap
Sorata, Bolivia
20th century
Wool; double-faced warp pattern, plain weave
stripes, tassels on side and bottom
28 ⅜ x 18 ½ in. (72 x 47 cm)
Collected by Grace Goodell, accessioned 1969
American Museum of Natural History, 40.1/3580

29

Coca bag with strap
Pocoata, Bolivia
20th century
Wool; double-faced warp pattern, braided strap
20 ⅞ x 7 ⅛ in. (53 x 18 cm)
Collected by Grace Goodell, accessioned 1969
American Museum of Natural History, 40.1/3572
See fig. 3.

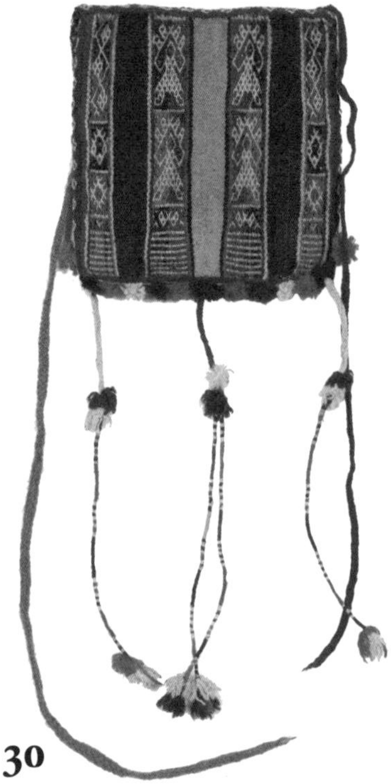

30

Coca bag
Atahuaycco, Bolivia
20th century
Wool; double-faced warp pattern, braided warp ends
32 ⅝ x 5 ⅞ in. (83 x 15 cm)
Collected by Grace Goodell, accessioned 1969
American Museum of Natural History, 40.1/3542

31

Set of two bags
Peru
2013
Synthetic fibers, wooden buttons; machine-made
6 ⅞ x 8 ⅞ in. (17.5 x 22.5 cm)
Purchased from Sanyork Fair Trade website
Private collection
See fig. 61.

32

"Tourist" *chuspa*
Arequipa, Peru
2013
Synthetic fibers, zipper, wooden buttons; machine-made, with embroidery
31 ⅞ x 11 in. (81 x 28 cm)
Purchased from vendor in tourist market
Private collection
See fig. 60.

33

"Mate Windsor" coca tea box
Peru
2011
Cardboard
3 x 5 ⅜ x 7 ⅞ in. (7.5 x 13.8 x 18.8 cm)
Private collection
See fig. 59.

Bibliography

Ackerman, Raquel. "Clothes and Identity in the Central Andes: Province of Abancay, Peru." In *Textile Traditions of Mesoamerica and the Andes: An Anthology*, edited by M. B. Schevill, J. C. Berlo, and E. B. Dwyer, 231–60. New York: Garland Publishing, 1991.

Acosta, Joseph de. *The Natural and Moral History of the Indies*. 1590. Reprint, London: Hakluyt Society, 1880.

Adavasio, James, and Thomas F. Lynch. "Pre-ceramic Textiles and Cordage from Guitarrero Cave, Peru." *American Antiquity* 38, no. 1 (1973): 84–90.

Adelson, Laurie, and Arthur Tracht. *Aymara Weavings: Ceremonial Textiles of Colonial and 19th Century Bolivia*. Washington, DC: Smithsonian Institution Traveling Service, 1983.

Allen, Catherine J. "To Be Quechua: The Symbolism of Coca Chewing in Highland Peru." *American Ethnologist* 8, no. 1 (1981): 157–71.

——. *The Hold Life Has: Coca and Cultural Identity in an Andean Community*. Washington, DC: Smithsonian Institution Press, 1988.

Appadurai, Arjun, ed. *The Social Life of Things: Commodities in Cultural Perspective*. Cambridge: Cambridge University Press, 1986.

Aufderheide, A. C. *The Scientific Study of Mummies*. Cambridge: Cambridge University Press, 2003.

Barraza Lescano, Sergio Alfredo. "Acllas y Personajes Emplumados en la Iconografía Alfarera Inca: una approximacion a la ritualidad prehispanica Andina." MA thesis, Pontifica Universidad Catolica del Peru, 2012.

Bergh, Susan E. "Tapestry-woven Tunics." In *Wari, Lords of the Ancient Andes*, edited by S. E. Bergh, 1–44. New York: Thames and Hudson, 2012.

Bertonio, P. Ludovico. *Vocabulario de la Lengua Aymara*. 1610. Reprint, Leipzig: B.G. Teubner, 1879.

Bird, Junius B. "Pre-Ceramic Art from Huaca Prieta, Chicama Valley." *Nawpa Pacha* 1 (1963): 29–34.

Bird, Junius B., John Hyslop, and Milica Dimitrijevic Skinner. *The Preceramic Excavations at the Huaca Prieta, Chicama Valley, Peru*. Vol. 62, Anthropological Papers of the American Museum of History. New York: American Museum of Natural History, 1985.

Bolton, Ralph. "Andean Coca Chewing: A Metabolic Perspective." *American Anthropologist* 78 (1976): 630–33.

Bray, Tamara, Leah D. Minc, Maria Constanza Ceruti, Jose Antonio Chavez, Ruddy Perea, and Johan Reinhard. "A Compositional Analysis of Pottery Vessels Associated with the Inca Ritual of Capacocha." *Journal of Anthropological Archaeology* 24 (2005): 82–100.

Bray, Warwick, and Colin Dollery. "Coca Chewing and High-Altitude Stress: A Spurious Correlation." *Current Anthropology* 24, no. 3 (1983): 269–82.

Burchard, Roderick E. "Coca y Trueque de Alimentos." In *Reciprocidad y Intercambio en los Andes Peruanos*, edited by G. Alberti and E. Mayer, 209–51. Lima: Instituto de Estudios Peruanos, 1974.

Burger, Richard L., and Lucy C. Salazar. *Machu Picchu: Unveiling the Mystery of the Incas*. New Haven and London: Yale University Press, 2004.

Caceres Santa Maria, Baldomero. "Historia, Prejucios y Version Psiquiatrica del Coqueo Andino." *Peru Indigena* 12, no. 28 (1990): 31–72.

Carmona Sciaraffia, Gabriela. "Los Nuevos Patrones Formales y Decorativos en Las Bolsas Chuspas del Area de Arica, Bajo el Dominio del Tawantisuyu: Una aproximacion inicial." In *XVII Congreso Nacional de Arqueologia Chilena: Actas I,* 26–27. Valdivia, Chile: Sociedad Chilena de Arqueologia, 2006.

Carter, William E., and Mauricio Mamani. *Coca en Bolivia.* La Paz, Bolivia: Libreria Editorial "Juventad," 1986.

Cartmell, Larry W., A. C. Aufderheide, Angela Springfield, Cheryl Weems, and Bernardo T. Arriaza. "The Frequency and Antiquity of Prehistoric Coca-Leaf-Chewing Practices in Northern Chile: Radioimmunoassay of a Cocaine Metabolite in Human-Mummy Hair." *Latin American Antiquity* 2, no. 3 (1991): 260–68.

Childe, V. Gordon. *Man Makes Himself.* New York: New American Library, 1951.

Chilton, Elizabeth S., ed. *Material Meanings: Critical Approaches to the Interpretation of Material Culture.* Salt Lake City: University of Utah Press, 1999.

Cieza de Leon, Pedro. *The Incas.* 1553. Translated by Harriet de Onis. Norman: University of Oklahoma Press, 1959.

Clark, Niki R. "The Estuquiña Textile Tradition: Cultural Patterning in Late Prehistoric Fabrics in Moquegua, Far Southern Peru." PhD diss., Washington University, 1993.

Cobo, Father Bernabe. *Inca Religion and Customs.* 1609. Translated by R. Hamilton. Austin: University of Texas Press, 1990.

Cohen, Mark Nathan. "Archaeological Plant Remains from the Central Coast of Peru." *Nawpa Pacha* 16 (1978): 23–50.

Conklin, William J. "Pucara and Tiahuanaco Tapestry: Time and Style in a Sierra Weaving Tradition." *Nawpa Pacha* 21 (1983): 1–44.

Costin, Cathy Lynne. "Housewives, Chosen Women, Skilled Men: Cloth Production and Social Identity in the Late Prehispanic Andes." In *Craft and Social Identity*, edited by C. L. Costin and R. P. Wright, 123–44. Arlington, VA: American Anthropological Association, 1998.

Cusack, John T. "The International Narcotics Control System: Coca and Cocaine." In *Coca and Cocaine: Effects on People and Policy in Latin America*, edited by D. Pacini and C. Franquemont, 65–71. Cambridge, MA: Cultural Survival, 1986.

D'Altroy, Terence N. *The Incas.* Malden, MA: Wiley-Blackwell, 2002.

Davidson, Kief, and Richard Ladkandi. *The Devil's Miner.* Film. Urban Lanscape Productions and La Mita Loca Films, 2005.

de Molina, Cristobal. *Account of the Fables and Rites of the Incas.* 1573. Translated by B. S. Bauer, V. Smith-Oka, and G. E. Cantarutti. Austin: University of Texas Press, 2011.

Demarest, Michael. "Cocaine: Middle Class High." *Time*, July 6, 1981.

DeMarrais, Elizabeth, Luis-Jaime Castillo, and Timothy K. Earle. "Ideology, Materialization and Power Strategies." *Current Anthropology* 37, no. 1 (1996): 15–31.

Engel, Frederich. "A Preceramic Settlement on the Central Coast of Peru: Asia, unit 1." *Transactions of the American Philosophical Society* 53, no. 3 (1963): 1–139.

Farthing, Linda. "Social Impacts Associated with Antidrug Law 1008." In *Coca, Cocaine, and the Bolivian Reality,* edited by M. B. Leons and H. Sanabria, 235–70. Albany: State University of New York Press, 1997.

Feltham, Jane. *Peruvian Textiles.* Aylesbury, UK: Shire Publications, 1989.

Femenias, Blenda. "Regional Dress of the Colca Valley, Peru: A Dynamic Tradition." In *Textile Traditions of Mesoamerica and the Andes: An Anthology*, edited by M. B. Schevill, J. C. Berlo, and E. B. Dwyer, 179–204. New York: Garland Publishing, 1991.

——. *Gender and the Boundaries of Dress in Contemporary Peru.* Austin: University of Texas Press, 2005.

Finley Hughes, Lauren. "Weaving Imperial Ideas: Iconography and Ideology of the Inca Coca Bag." *Textile* 8, no. 1 (2010): 148–79.

Frame, Mary. "What the Women Were Wearing: A Deposit of Early Nazca Dresses and Shawls from Cahuachi, Peru." *Textile Museum Journal* 42 (2003): 13–53.

Freed, Stanley A. *Anthropology Unmasked: Museums, Science, and Politics in New York City*. Vol. 2. Wilmington, OH: Orange Frazer Press, 2012.

Gagliano, Joseph A. "The Coca Debate in Colonial Peru." *The Americas* 20, no. 1 (1963): 43–63.

———. "Coca and Popular Medicine in Peru: An Historical Analysis of Attitudes." In *Medical Anthropology: Pre-Congress Conference of Medical Anthropology, Stitch School of Medicine 1973*, edited by F. X. Grollig and H. B. Haley, 49–66. The Hague: Mouton Publishers, 1976.

Gavilan Ramos, Alonso. *Historia de Copacabana y de la Milagrosa Imagen de su Virgen*. 1621. Reprint, La Paz: La Union Catolica, 1886.

Gifford, Douglas, and Paulin Hoggarth. *Carnival and Coca Leaf: Some Traditions of the Peruvian Quechua Ayllu*. New York: St. Martin's Press, 1976.

Goldstein, Paul S. *Andean Diaspora: The Tiwanaku Colonies and the Origins of South American Empire*. Gainesville: University Press of Florida, 2005.

Gootenberg, Paul. "Between Coca and Cocaine: A Century or More of U.S.–Peruvian Drug Paradoxes, 1860–1980." *Hispanic American Historical Review* 83, no. 1 (2003): 119–50.

———. "Secret Ingredients: The Politics of Coca in US–Peruvian Relations, 1915–65." *Journal of Latin American Studies* 36, no. 2 (2004): 233–65.

———. "Cocaine in Chains: The Rise and Demise of a Global Commodity, 1860–1950." In *From Silver to Cocaine: Latin American Commodity Chains and the Building of the World Economy, 1500–2000*, edited by S. Topik, C. Marichal, and Z. Frank, 321–51. Durham, NC: Duke University Press, 2006.

Guaman Poma de Ayala, Felipe. *The First New Chronicle and Good Government: On the History of the World and the Incas up to 1615*. 1615. Reprint, Austin: University of Texas Press, 2009.

Gutierrez-Noriega, Carlos, and Victor Wolfgang von Hagen. "Coca: The Mainstay of an Arduous Native Life in the Andes." *Economic Botany* 5, no. 2 (1951): 145–52.

Hanna, Joel M. "Further Studies of the Effects of Coca Chewing on Exercise." *Human Biology* 43 (1971): 200–209.

———. "Responses of Quechua Indians to Coca Ingestion during Cold Exposure." *American Journal of Physical Anthropology* 34 (1971): 273–78.

———. "Coca Leaf Use in Southern Peru: Some Biosocial Aspects." *American Anthropologist* 76, no. 2 (1974): 281–96.

Hastorf, Christine A. "Archaeological Evidence of Coca (*Erythroxylum coca*, Erythroxylaceae) in the Upper Mantaro Valley, Peru." *Economic Botany* 41, no. 2 (1987): 292–301.

Healy, Kevin. *Llamas, Weavings and Organic Chocolate: Multicultural Grassroots Development in the Andes and Amazon of Bolivia*. South Bend, IN: University of Notre Dame Press, 2001.

Heckman, Andrea M. *Woven Stories: Andean Textiles and Rituals*. Albuquerque: University of New Mexico Press, 2003.

Hodder, Ian, ed. *The Archaeology of Contextual Meanings*. Cambridge: Cambridge University Press, 1987.

———. *The Meaning of Things: Material Culture and Symbolic Expression*. London: Unwin Hyman, 1989.

Horta, Helena, and Carolina Aguero. "Definicion de Chuspa: Textil de Uso Ritual durante el Periodo Intermedio Tardio, en la Zona Arqueologica de Arica." In *Actas XIV Congreso Nacional de Arqueologia Chilena*, 48. Copiapo, Chile: Museo Regional de Atacama, 1999.

Hurcombe, Linda. *Archaeological Artifacts as Material Culture*. London: Routledge, 2007.

Indriati, Etty, and Jane E Buikstra. "Coca Chewing in Prehistoric Coastal Peru: Dental Evidence." *American Journal of Physical Anthropology* 114 (2001): 242–57.

Isbell, Billie Jean. *To Defend Ourselves: Ecology and Ritual in an Andean Village*. Prospect Heights, IL: Waveland Press, 1978.

Jolie, Edward, Thomas F. Lynch, Phil R. Geib, and James Adavasio. "Cordage, Textiles, and the Late Pleistocene Peopling of the Andes." *Current Anthropology* 52, no. 2 (2011): 285–96.

Karch, Steven B. *A Brief History of Cocaine*. Boca Raton, FL: CRC Press, 1997.

Kay, Bruce H. "Violent Opportunities: The Rise and Fall of 'King Coca' and Shining Path." *Journal of Interamerican Studies and World Affairs* 41, no. 3 (1999): 97–127.

Keefe, Patrick Radden. "Cocaine Incorporated." *New York Times*, June 15, 2012.

Kernaghan, Richard. *Coca's Gone: Of Might and Right in the Huallaga Post-Boom*. Stanford: Stanford University Press, 2009.

King, Heidi, ed. *Peruvian Featherworks: Art of the Precolumbian Era*. New York: The Metropolitan Museum of Art, 2012.

Klepinger, Linda L., John K. Kuhn, and Josephus Thomas Jr. "Prehistoric Dental Calculus Gives Evidence for Coca in Early Coastal Ecuador." *Nature* 269 (1977): 506–7.

Korpisaari, Antti, and Martti Parssinen. *Pariti: The Ceremonial Tiwanaku Pottery of an Island in Lake Titicaca*. Helsinki: Academia Scientiarum Fennica, 2011.

Kroeber, Alfred L., and Donald Collier. *The Archaeology and Pottery of Nazca, Peru: Alfred Kroeber's 1926 Expedition*, edited by P. Carmichael. Walnut Creek, CA: Alta Mira Press, 1998.

La Barre, Weston. *The Aymara Indians of the Lake Titicaca Plateau, Bolivia*. Arlington, VA: American Anthropological Association, 1948.

Landes, Alejandro. *Cocalero*. Film. New York: First Run Features, 2007.

Lathrap, Donald, Donald Collier, and Helen Chandra. *Ancient Ecuador: Culture, Clay and Creativity 3000–300 B.C.* Chicago: Field Museum of Natural History, 1975.

Lumbreras, Luis G., and H. Amat. "Secuencia arqueologica del altiplano occidental del Titicaca." Paper presented at 37 Congreso Internacional de Americanistas, Stuttgart, Germany, August 11–18, 1968.

Mariani, Angelo. *Coca and Its Therapeutic Application*. 2nd ed. New York: J. N. Jaros, 1892.

Markham, Clements R. *Travels in Peru and India*. London: John Murray, 1862.

Martindale, William. *Coca and Cocaine: Their History, Medical and Economic Uses, and Medicinal Preparations*. London: H. K. Lewis, 1894.

Meisch, Lynn A. "We Are Sons of Atahualpa and We Will Win: Traditional Dress in Otavalo and Saraguro, Ecuador." In *Textile Traditions of Mesoamerica and the Andes: An Anthology*, edited by M. B. Schevill, J. C. Berlo, and E. B. Dwyer, 145–77. New York: Garland Publishing, 1991.

Mortimer, W. Golden. *History of Coca: "The Divine Plant" of the Incas*. 1901. Reprint, San Francisco: Fitz Hugh Ludlow Memorial Library, 1974.

Moseley, Michael E. *The Incas and Their Ancestors: The Archaeology of Peru*. 2nd ed. London: Thames and Hudson, 2001.

Murra, John V. *The Economic Organization of the Inca State, Research in Economic Anthropology*. Greenwich, CT: JAI Press Inc., 1980.

——. "Notes on Pre-Columbian Cultivation of Coca Leaf." In *Coca and Cocaine: Effects on People and Policy in Latin America*, edited by D. Pacini and C. Franquemont, 49–52. Cambridge, MA: Cultural Survival, 1986.

Oakland, Amy Rodman. "Textiles and Ethnicity: Tiwanaku in San Pedro de Atacama, North Chile." *Latin American Antiquity* 3, no. 4 (1992): 316–40.

——. "Weaving in a High Land: A Continuous Tradition." In *Traditional Textiles of the Andes: Life and Cloth in the Highlands*, edited by L. A. Meisch, 16–27. London: Thames and Hudson, 1997.

Pacini, Deborah, and Christine Franquemont. *Coca and Cocaine: Effects on People and Policy in Latin America*. Vol. 23, Cultural Survival Report. Cambridge, MA: Cultural Survival, 1986.

Paly, D., P. Jatlow, C. Van Dyke, F. Cabieses, and R. Byck. "Plasma Levels of Cocaine in Native Peruvian Coca Chewers." In *Cocaine 1980: Proceedings of the Interamerican Seminar on Coca and Cocaine*, edited by F. R. Jeri, 86–89. Lima: Pacific Press, 1980.

Patterson, T. C. "Central Peru: Its Population and Economy." *Archaeology* 24 (1971): 316–21.

Paul, Anne. *Paracas Ritual Attire: Symbols of Authority in Ancient Peru.* Norman: University of Oklahoma Press, 1990.

Phipps, Elena. "Garments and Identity in the Colonial Andes." In *The Colonial Andes: Tapestries and Silverwork, 1530–1830,* edited by E. Phipps, J. Hecht, and C. Esteras Martin, 17–39. New York: The Metropolitan Museum of Art, 2004.

——. *Looking at Textiles: A Guide to Technical Terms.* Los Angeles: The J. Paul Getty Museum, 2011.

Phipps, Elena, Joanna Hecht, and Cristina Esteras Martin, eds. *The Colonial Andes: Tapestries and Silverwork, 1530–1830.* New York: The Metropolitan Museum of Art, 2004.

Plowman, Timothy. "Botanical Perspectives on Coca." *Journal of Psychedelic Drugs* 11, nos. 1–2 (1979): 103–17.

——. "The Ethnobotany of Coca (Erythroxylum spp., Erythroxylaceae)." In *Ethnobotany in the Neotropics,* edited by G. T. Prance and J. A. Kallunki, 62–111. New York: The New York Botanical Garden, 1984.

——. "The Origin, Evolution, and Diffusion of Coca, *Erythroxylum* spp., in South and Central America." In *Pre-Columbian Plant Migration,* edited by D. Stone, 125–64. Cambridge, MA: Peabody Museum of Archaeology and Ethnology, 1984.

Presta, Ana Maria. "Undressing the Coya and Dressing the Indian Woman: Market Economy, Clothing and Identities in the Colonial Andes, La Plata (Charcas), Late Sixteenth and Early Seventeenth Centuries." *Hispanic American Historical Review* 90, no. 1 (2009): 41–74.

Quijada Jara, Sergio. *La Coca en las Costumbres Indigenas.* Huancayo, Peru: CIUSAL, 1950.

Raimondi, Antonio. *El Peru.* Vol. 1. Lima: Imprenta del Estado, 1874.

Reinhard, Johan, and Maria Constanza Ceruti. *Inca Rituals and Sacred Mountains: A Study of the World's Highest Archaeological Sites.* Los Angeles: Cotsen Institute of Archaeology Press, 2010.

Renfrew, Colin, and Paul Bahn. *Archaeology: Theories, Methods and Practice.* 2nd ed. London: Thames and Hudson, 1996.

Rexer, Lyle, and Rachel Klein. *American Museum of Natural History: 125 Years of Expedition and Discovery.* New York: Harry N. Abrams, 1995.

Roel Mendizabal, Pedro, and Paola Borja Chavez. *Anaco de Camilaca: Uso contemporaneo de un traje prehispanico.* Lima, Peru: Ministerio de Cultura de Peru, 2011.

Rostworowski de Diez Canseco, Maria. *Plantaciones Prehispanicas de Coca en la Vertiente del Pacifico.* Lima, Peru: IEP Instituto de Estudios Peruanos, 1989.

Rowe, Ann Pollard. "Inca Weaving and Costume." *Textile Museum Journal* 34 (1995): 5–54.

——. "The Art of Peruvian Textiles." In *Andean Art at Dumbarton Oaks,* edited by E. Hill Boone, 329–45. Washington, DC: Dumbarton Oaks Research Library and Collection, 1996.

Rowe, Ann Pollard, and John Cohen. *Hidden Threads of Peru: Q'ero Textiles.* Washington, DC: Merrell, in association with The Textile Museum, 2002.

Sanabria, Harry. "The Discourse and Practice of Repression and Resistance in the Chapare." In *Coca, Cocaine, and the Bolivian Reality,* edited by M. B. Leons and H. Sanabria, 169–94. Albany: State University of New York Press, 1997.

Sarmiento de Gamboa, Pedro. *History of the Incas.* 1572. Mineola, NY: Dover Publications, 1999.

——. *The History of the Incas.* 1572. Translated by B. S. Bauer and V. Smith. Austin: University of Texas Press, 2007.

Silverman, Helaine. "Touring Ancient Times: The Present and Presented Past in Contemporary Peru." *American Anthropologist* 104, no. 3 (2002): 881–902.

Spedding, Alison L. "Cocataki, Taki-Coca: Trade, Traffic, and Organized Peasant Resistance in the Yungas of La Paz." In *Coca, Cocaine, and the Bolivian Reality,* edited by M. B. Leons and H. Sanabria, 117–38. Albany: State University of New York Press, 1997.

Stafford, Cora. *Paracas Embroideries: A Study of Repeated Patterns.* New York: J. J. Augustin, 1941.

Ubelaker, Douglas H., and Karen E. Stothert. "Elemental Analysis of Alkalis and Dental Deposits Associated with Coca Chewing in Ecuador." *Latin American Antiquity* 17, no. 1 (2006): 77–89.

United Nations Office on Drugs and Crime. *Single Convention on Narcotic Drugs*. New York: UNODC, 1961.

Vallejos, M. "Analisis y tipologia de los textiles de Paloma: un pueblo de 7000 anos en las lomas de Chilca, Peru." *Revista del Museo Nacional de Antropologia y Arqueologia* 3 (1988): 6–37.

Vanstan, Ina. *Textiles from Beneath the Temple at Pachacamac, Peru: A Part of the Uhle Collection of the University Museum, University of Pennsylvania*. Philadelphia: The University Museum, University of Pennsylvania, 1967.

von Tschudi, John James. *Travels in Peru: On the Coast, in the Sierra, across the Cordilleras and the Andes, into the Primeval Forests*. Translated by T. Ross. New York: A. S. Barnes, 1854.

Wallert, Arie, and Ran Boytner. "Dyes from the Tumilaca and Chiribaya Cultures, South Coast of Peru." *Journal of Archaeological Science* 23 (1996): 853–61.

Zorn, Elayne. *Weaving a Future: Tourism, Cloth, and Culture on an Andean Island*. Iowa City: University of Iowa Press, 2008.

Zuidema, R. T. "Hierarchy and Space in Incaic Social Organization." *Ethnohistory* 30, no. 2 (1983): 49–75.

Index

Page numbers in italics indicate maps,
illustrations, and photographs.

This catalogue is published in conjunction with the exhibition *Carrying Coca: 1,500 Years of Andean Chuspas* held at the Bard Graduate Center: Decorative Arts, Design History, Material Culture from April 11 through August 3, 2014.

Curator of the exhibition: Nicola Sharratt

Focus Gallery team:
Head of Focus Gallery Project: Ivan Gaskell
Chief Curator: Marianne Lamonaca
Focus Gallery Project coordinator:
Ann Marguerite Tartsinis
Exhibition designer: Ian Sullivan
Director of the Digital Media Lab:
Kimon Keramidas
Dean for Academic Administration and
Student Affairs: Elena Pinto Simon

Catalogue production:
Director, Bard Graduate Center Gallery and
Gallery Publications: Nina Stritzler-Levine
Coordinator, catalogue production:
Ann Marguerite Tartsinis
Catalogue design and production:
Kate DeWitt with Erica Lai
Coordinator of catalogue photography:
Alexis Mucha
Copy editor: Barbara Burn

Published by Bard Graduate Center:
Decorative Arts, Design History, Material
Culture, New York

Cover:
Grace Goodell. Detail, men and boys in a market, Bolivia, 1968. Courtesy of the Division of Anthropology, American Museum of Natural History. Fig. 45.

Frontispiece:
Felipe Guaman Poma de Ayala. "Governor of the Provinces," page 348, drawing 136. From *El primer nueva corónica y buen gobierno*, 1615–16. Det Kongelige Bibliotek, Copenhagen, Denmark. Fig. 16.

Page 4:
Coca bag. Q'ero Village, Department of Cuzco, Peru, accessioned in 1956. Wool; three-warp patterned straps with *inti* motifs; three small pockets woven into the principal bag as part of the pattern. Courtesy of the Division of Anthropology, American Museum of Natural History, 40.0/8907. Cat. 5.

Page 6:
Detail, coca bag. Atahuaycco, Bolivia, 20th century. Wool; double-faced warp pattern, braided warp ends. Collected by Grace Goodell, accessioned 1969, American Museum of Natural History, 40.1/3542.

Typeface:
This book is set in *Espinosa Nova* (Cristóbal Henestrosa, 2010) based on the typefaces used by the sixteenth-century Mexican printer Antonio de Espinosa.

Exclusive trade distribution by Yale University Press, New Haven and London
ISBN (Yale University Press): 978-0-300-20072-0

Library of Congress Cataloging-in-Publication Data

Sharratt, Nicola.
Carrying coca : 1,500 years of Andean *chuspas* / Nicola Sharratt. — First edition.
pages cm.
Includes bibliographical references and index.
ISBN 978-0-300-20072-0 (pbk.)
1. Indian textile fabrics—Andes Region. 2. Indians of South America—Drug use—Andes Region.
3. Indians of South America—Rites and ceremonies. 4. Coca—Social aspects—Andes Region. 5. Andes Region—Social life and customs.
6. Andes Region—Religious life and customs.
I. Title.
  F2230.1.D78S53 2014
  980—dc23
                              2013044787

Printed by GHP, West Haven, Connecticut